DATE DUE		

PRINCIPLES OF LITERARY
CRITICISM

PRINCIPLES OF
LITERARY CRITICISM

By

Prof. LASCELLES ABERCROMBIE
Professor of English Literature in the
University of London

GREENWOOD PRESS, PUBLISHERS
WESTPORT, CONNECTICUT

Library of Congress Cataloging in Publication Data

Abercrombie, Lascelles, 1881-1938.
Principles of literary criticism.

Reprint of the 1932 ed. published by V. Gollancz,
London.
Bibliography: p.
1. Criticism--History. I. Title.
[PN86.A23   1979]   801'.95   78-21288
ISBN 0-313-20025-4

This edition published in 1932 by Victor Gollancz Ltd.,
London

Reprinted with the permission of the Estate of Lascelles
Abercrombie.

Reprinted in 1979 by Greenwood Press, Inc.
51 Riverside Avenue, Westport, CT 06880

Printed in the United States of America

10 9 8 7 6 5 4 3 2 1

CONTENTS

I. INTRODUCTORY

WHEN SOCRATES was explaining to his judges how it was that he had made himself so unpopular, he told them of his investigations into the wisdom of those whom the world reputed to be wise. The enquiry had been strangely disappointing ; and when he came to describe his encounter with the poets, " Gentlemen," he said, " I am ashamed to tell you the truth. I took the poems which seemed to be most carefully composed "—the suggestion is, that these were the poems in which the poets ought to have been most conscious of what they were doing—" and I asked them what they meant." But the poets could not tell him that : " There was scarcely a man present "—for it seems these interrogations took place in the presence of the poets' admirers—" who could not talk about these poems much better than the poets themselves."

Socrates had, in fact, made a discovery of first-rate importance. With the peculiar and characteristic turn he gave to his discovery, we are not now concerned. The thing for us to note is, that he was the first person to distinguish between the ability to criticize literature and the ability to compose it. " I soon found out," he said, " that poets do not compose poetry because they are wise, but because they have a certain nature or genius, which is capable of enthusiasm,"—or, as we might nowadays put it, of being inspired ; poets in this respect being, he went on, " like prophets and oracular persons, who also say many fine things without knowing what it is they are saying." When he invited the poets to tell him what their poems " meant," Socrates was testing them for what he called " wisdom " : that is to say, for the power of rational analysis conducted in strict accordance with definite intellectual principles. In other words, he was inviting them to criticize their own poems. He found them unable to do so.

If it had suited his purpose, Socrates might have gone on to point out that the power to enjoy poetry is also quite different from the power to analyse it rationally. The power to enjoy poetry, like the power to compose it, proceeds from a certain nature. Very probably, indeed, both powers proceed from the same nature ; only in the one case it exists passively, in the other actively. Nevertheless, the two powers themselves are obviously quite distinct. And now to these must be added a third power—the power to criticize literature. For when Socrates interrogated the poets, he was not putting impertinent or unnecessary questions. Ever since man became conscious of possessing in the art of literature a region in which he could exercise some of his most delightful and most profitable energies, people have not only been asking what poems " meant," but all sorts of other questions as well, which properly fall under the heading of criticism. What makes Socrates' " Apology " the first milestone in the history of criticism is simply this : that there Socrates for the first time clearly pointed out that criticism is a distinct species of literary activity, and also why it is distinct.

We may say, then, that the realm of literature is occupied by the activities of three distinct powers : the power to create, the power to enjoy, and the power to criticize. The chief thing that distinguishes the power to criticize from the other two is the fact that it can be acquired. For, though criticism may be intuitive, the critic may also be conscious of the process by which he criticizes ; and this process appeals to certain intellectual principles which can be set out in an orderly system, studied, and deliberately put into practice. But there are no principles which will tell you how to create literature, nor how to enjoy it. Criticism, then, does not pretend to account for the state of mind in which literature is created, nor for that in which it is enjoyed : still less does it pretend to bring these states of mind into existence if they do not exist already. It assumes their existence : for the person who can neither create nor enjoy literature, all criticism must be entirely meaningless. That is to say, it assumes the fact that literature exists ; and it then proceeds to enquire into the nature of that fact, to expound it, to assess its value, and in a word to think clearly about it.

And this, as Socrates pointed out, is quite distinct from the power to create literature, and, as he might have pointed out, quite distinct also from the power to enjoy it. Nevertheless, though perfectly distinguishable, it can co-exist with either

of the other two powers. Socrates may
have been unlucky in his poets : not all
the poets living in his day, one imagines,
would have been incapable of telling him
what their poems " meant." Perhaps those
whom he questioned found it a little difficult to make out what Socrates himself
" meant " when he asked them what their
poems " meant " ; perhaps they thought
it a sufficient answer to say, that what a
poem means is simply—itself. No doubt
there is such a thing as quite uncritical
composition in literature ; no doubt there
is such a thing as quite uncritical enjoyment. But both must be very rare. As soon
as a man becomes aware that it would suit
his purpose to say a thing this way rather
than that, as soon as a man becomes
aware that he likes this thing better than
that, criticism begins : which is as much
as to say, that criticism begins when
literature begins. But criticism as a noticeable activity in literature begins when
vague instinctive preference passes into
consciously defined choice which can be
rationally justified : when, that is to say,
there is an appeal to intellectual principles.
What is to be gained by such an appeal ?
Ultimately, simply this : the gain of being

intelligent. Whatever man can think about at all, some men will insist on thinking about with the most conscientious precision and lucidity that can be contrived. But there is a more obvious reward. Criticism enables the man who has the energy to create literature, to make the most intelligent, and therefore the most efficient, use of his energy ; and just so criticism enables the man who has the capacity to enjoy literature, to make his enjoyment the most intelligent, and therefore the most discriminating and most illuminating, kind of experience.

Criticism, as distinct from creation and enjoyment, consists in asking and answering rational questions about literature. These questions are of two main kinds, according as they proceed from literature in general to particular pieces of literature, or the other way round. In the first kind of enquiry we regard literature as a certain class of things, and we ask how it is that we are able to take this general view of literature as a whole. What does the word " literature " mean ? What are the properties common to all literature, by reason of which it exists as such ? Above all, what is the function of literature ? The results of this enquiry can be set out in a system of principles which expresses our understanding of the nature of literature. It is important to note that last point. These principles are intellectual principles ; but they are not principles which the intellect lays down *a priori* as prescribing the nature which literature *ought* to have. The nature of literature is a fact which exists, whether we investigate it or not, like any other objective fact. The principles of literature are the answers which our intellect gives us when we ask what sort of a fact literature is.

This kind of enquiry may be called the theory of literature. It only touches incidentally or by illustration on the merits of particular pieces of literature. On the contrary, the merit of this or that particular piece of literature is precisely the topic of the second main kind of enquiry. This is what usually goes under the name of criticism, and may indeed be called criticism proper. The question here is, not of literature in general, but of unique qualities in actual concrete examples of literature : what are the qualities which give to some particular work its peculiar individuality, and whether these are good

or bad qualities. Style, in the broadest
sense, which includes mood and spirit and
the choice of matter as well as technique
and language, is the subject of criticism
proper ; and its end is to assess literary
merit. Only incidentally to this does it
touch on the function of literature.

Strictly speaking, the theory of literature
belongs to that department of philosophy
which is called æsthetics. But the two kinds
of enquiry cannot be kept apart ; indeed,
no clear line can be drawn between them.
The theory of literature must be continually referring to the fact of literature ;
which means, it must be continually referring to actual specimens of literature ;
and to a considerable degree, these instances will be helpful according to the
literary merit they possess. On the other
hand, criticism proper naturally prefers to
stand on something more reliable than
impressions which may be at the mercy of
personal prejudices or emotional accidents.
The history of criticism has been very
largely the history of attempts to formulate rules for criticism, chiefly by compar-
ing the merits of several similar works
of literature, and the means used to produce them. But rules derived from some

particular instances in one kind of literature do not give the security required. Over and over again, such rules have been found wanting. When the number of instances has been enlarged, the rules have broken down. Thus, critics have demanded that epic poems should have invocations or funeral games or supernatural machinery, simply because these qualities occur in several good instances. So too the brilliant success of French classical drama induced many critics to accept the rule that drama should observe the unities of time and place. And however many particular instances the rules may be enlarged to include, they can never be safe rules, so long as they are derived from the comparison of meritorious qualities, and not from the intellectual principles of the theory of literature. For you can never be sure that such qualities, however meritorious, are essential. Only the principles which express the nature, and define the function, of literature in general can determine what is essential in any kind of literature ; and only by appealing to what is essential can criticism provide itself with trustworthy rules.

Thus the two kinds of rational enquiry

in literature, which we have called the theory of literature and criticism proper, necessarily overlap. Neither can complete itself without involving the other. Even if we confine the word criticism to the assessment of merit, there can be no security in this unless its analysis can appeal to intellectual principles. For our purposes, therefore, it is right to include the theory of literature under the heading of criticism. We shall proceed by discussing several works of outstanding importance in the history of criticism, whether their motive was philosophical (the theory of literature) or æsthetic (criticism proper). A complete history of European criticism cannot be attempted. Our attention will be chiefly given to those philosophical treatises which are especially valuable to æsthetic criticism, and to some critical enquiries important in the process of English literature. The chief place will be occupied by a discussion of the first and most celebrated of all systematic theories of literature, Aristotle's *Poetics*. We shall discuss this great treatise, not for the way it exemplifies the culture in which it originated, but for its contribution to all subsequent culture. And we shall discuss it at length because in it Aristotle raises almost all the problems out of which emerge the principles required by criticism for its security. Aristotle does not always solve these problems satisfactorily ; but he compels us to consider them exactly. But first of all it will be advisable to take a general view of the rational examination of literature.

II. THE ART OF LITERATURE

II. THE ART OF LITERATURE

LITERATURE is an art by which expression is achieved in language. As a preliminary description, that statement will do well enough ; but it is evidently inadequate as a definition of literature. Not everything which might come under that description would be called literature—not, at least, if the word literature is to retain any precision of meaning : and when we allow a word to become vague in its meaning, we deprive it of its usefulness. Thus, conversation is not literature ; and yet we speak of the art of conversation. The word *art*, in fact, appears to have many meanings : besides the so-called fine arts, we speak of the art of cooking, the art of war, the art of advertising, and a hundred other arts. But the word has the same core of meaning in all its contexts : it is always skill definitely and deliberately designed to produce an intended result. Clearly, then, we cannot rely on the word *art* to define what we mean by literature ; if we attempted to do so, we should only beg the question, and say, in effect, that art here means the art which produces literature. On the contrary, we can only define what we mean by art here when we know what we mean by literature. Certainly, there are degrees of skill; we may easily admit, that in literature there is a higher degree of verbal skill—more studied, more consistent, more intent—than in conversation. Moreover, in literature, the skill is *only* in words : in conversation, the skill is also in the use of personality—sometimes more than in the use of words. Poetry may be recited, of course, and plays may be acted; but the literary art is substantially the same whether it is spoken aloud or read in silence.

We must not, therefore, define literature by referring it to the written or printed word. For the word intelligible to the eye is only the symbol of the word intelligible to the ear ; and is in fact *heard* (though it may be only mentally) at the same time that it is visually read. Moreover, in a great deal of literature—in all poetry, for instance—it is as essential to the art of it that the words should be vividly heard (though, once more, they need be only mentally heard) as that they should be understood.

22

Precisely what we mean by art in the case of literature, then, must be left to appear as we narrow down the idea of literature. Art, we say, is skill designed to produce an intended result. What is the result aimed at in the art of literature? We have described literature as a species of expression. But this is only one side of the business. Literature exists not only in expressing a thing ; it equally exists in the receiving of the thing expressed. If I tell you of something I have experienced, my words, on my side, *express* my experience ; but on your side, my words *represent* my experience. It would be just as true, therefore, to say that literature represents things as to say that it expresses things. The possibility of regarding literature in either of these two directions has influenced not merely criticism, but literature itself. To regard literature as the expression of its author's mind (or mood or temperament) emphasizes the subjective element in it, and thus leads ultimately to romanticism ; in which what the author felt is the important thing. The opposite way of regarding literature, as a method of representing things to the reader, emphasizes the objective element, and thus leads ultimately to realism ; in which the substance exhibited is the important thing. Both of these aspects are true ; but neither is the whole truth. For the theory of literature, we require a word that will include both these aspects on equal terms ; and the simple word *communication* will give us exactly what we want. For evidently, whatever else literature may be, communication it must be : no communication, no literature. Though we are apt to speak as if the mere existence of a piece of language could constitute literary art, we must always remember that language is only the medium of the art. The art consists in the communication established between author and reader (or, of course, hearer). Clearly, then, what we mean by literature will be given by the *kind* of communication which this art sets up.

When we speak of the art of literature, then, we imply the existence of a series of three terms : the two extremes are author and reader ; the middle term is language. That is what it means to say literature is communication. But we need not banish the words *expression* and *representation* (or *imitation*, which contains the same notion

24

as the latter word : of imitation we shall hear much later on). On the contrary, they are often very useful words ; *expression* especially useful just now, when the question must unavoidably be, what kind of communication does literature set up between author and reader ? But whenever we use them, it will always be understood, that expression has achieved a form *communicable* to another mind, and that representation has arrived by being *communicated* from another mind. The importance of this, in the theory of literature, can hardly be exaggerated.

We are at once struck, when we survey the studied and deliberate use of language, by the fact that sometimes we can approve of the language for the way it conveys something the worth of which can be judged quite apart from the language ; and sometimes our approval of the thing conveyed cannot be distinguished from our approval of the language conveying it. In either case, we have an art. But in the first case, we have an art which exists for the sake of something justifiable outside the art itself ; in the other case, we have an art which exists, as it seems, simply for the sake of existing as art. The first we may call *applied art*, the second *pure art* ; and we may illustrate the difference by contrasting *The Origin of Species* with the *Ode on a Grecian Urn*. Both Darwin and Keats, we may say, wrote in order to express themselves. But Darwin expressed himself for the purpose of putting his readers in possession of a certain body of information, and of thereby persuading them of the cogency of a certain line of argument. We judge his power of expressing himself as it enabled him to achieve these purposes ; but we do not judge these purposes by his power of expressing himself. We ask whether the information is true, whether the argument is reasonable ; the virtue of the expression consists in the way it enables us to ask these questions, to make these judgements. If the expression were clumsy, the information might nevertheless still be true and the argument reasonable ; but it might be more difficult to arrive at these judgements. The purpose of *The Origin of Species*, then, is *served* by the literary quality of the book (" literary quality " meaning, at present, according to our preliminary description, simply expressive power) ; but it is not *justified* by this literary quality. We can distinguish,

26

therefore, the merit of Darwin's purpose from the merit of his expressive power.

But in the *Ode on a Grecian Urn*, what purpose can be distinguished from its expression? It offers us no information which may or may not be true, no argument which may or may not be reasonable ; neither are we invited to consider whether it is useful or moral. This is expression which satisfies us simply by existing as expression. The art here does not conduct us to a position from which we can judge of something outside the art ; this is art which serves no purpose but to be itself, and which prompts us to judge of nothing but of itself as art. In this sense the art is pure ; and when we speak of literature, we either mean that the art is in this sense pure, or that we are regarding it as in this sense pure. For it is possible to consider *The Origin of Species* as literature ; but only by attending to Darwin's power of expression as such, disregarding or taking for granted the purpose he aimed at. The case would be even clearer in a work of history. It is, in fact, very easy to read, say, Gibbon's *Decline and Fall of the Roman Empire* without much concern for the accuracy of his facts or the justice of his interpretation, taking it merely as a magnificent pomp of events presented to the imagination. If we do so, we take it as a work of pure literature, expression justified simply as such. Thus, by *applied literature*, we mean work which can be regarded as literature by ignoring its author's purpose : what he intended as a means to an end, we take as an end in itself. But in *pure literature* no such exclusion of the author's purpose is required ; for there never was any purpose except that the expression should exist for the mere sake of existing as itself. Our discussion of the art of literature, then, will concern itself wholly with pure literature, with the expression which justifies itself by the mere fact of existing. Whenever we speak of literature, we shall mean pure literature. Applied literature we shall ignore—anything which was written to give information or to make argument persuasive, any expression designed to serve a purpose beyond the mere achievement of expression as such. We shall ignore all this for two reasons. First, because whatever expressive qualities may be found in applied literature, may be much more easily and more demonstrably found in pure literature,

28

along with a much greater range of such qualities. Secondly, because the principles to which criticism of these expressive qualities must appeal will most naturally reveal themselves when expression has to rely solely on itself for all its justification, being actuated by no other purpose than to exist as such.

But when we say the art of literature is expression, we mean communicable expression : more precisely, we mean that the artist, in expressing himself, communicates with someone else. What does he communicate ? In the case of Darwin, the answer is obvious ; he gives us facts, and a theory. But what does Keats communicate? When expression justifies itself simply by existing as such, what is communicated then ? The answer can only be, something which, unlike Darwin's message, justifies itself simply by being communicated. And if we go on to ask, what sort of a thing is that ? again there is only one answer : *experience*—experience which is accepted and valued simply because it is experience. So accepted, we may call it *pure experience*. The epithet really adds nothing ; for by the very nature of experience, it can never be anything but purely itself. But we are

29

not always satisfied to take experience at its face-value. We may ask whether it is true or reasonable or useful or moral. If I am looking at a landscape, I may, if I am a farmer, judge what I see in accordance with familiar practical values : I may ask myself whether I am looking at good farming land. On the other hand, I may be perfectly satisfied with the experience of looking at the landscape without asking any questions about it at all. I am merely aware that the landscape is *beautiful*. And whenever I am aware of that, I experience something which is wholly satisfactory by the mere fact of being experienced. Now if I express this, my expression of it will have no purpose but to exist as such ; and if my expression is communicable in language, I shall have achieved literature : I shall have communicated something which can be satisfactory simply because it has been communicated.

The matter of literature, then, is pure experience. This puts no restriction on the scope of literature. Nothing can happen in life that cannot be taken as experience valued for its own immediate sake. Though we are not always satisfied to accept experience at its face-value, it is always possible to be so satisfied, provided the experience is comprehensible. The possibility of pure experience in sensuous or emotional life is obvious ; but it is equally possible in intellectual or any other life. We can enter into and enjoy a train of reasoning simply as an intellectual experience, whether we are convinced by it or not. There are few things more satisfactory in themselves, more supremely beautiful, than the structure of Spinoza's philosophy : but its beauty is one thing, its truth is another. Who indeed can tell whether it is true ? But anyone who can understand it can know its beauty. And how often in literature do we not accept moral or religious conditions which we would never think of accepting in real life ? We accept them simply as experiences. Even when we experience something which we feel bound to judge, not at its face-value, but for its truth or reasonableness, its morality or utility, the very act of so judging it can be intuited as experience, and enjoyed for its own sake. Thus, wherever there is life, there is the possibility of pure experience, and so of literature. This gives another explanation of applied literature. We have seen that

The Origin of Species can be regarded as literature if we ignore Darwin's purpose, and simply regard for its own sake the expression he designed to serve his purpose. But besides excluding the author's purpose, we may also transform it : that is to say, we may take it as an enjoyable exhibition of purpose. That is how Spinoza's *Ethics* may be regarded as literature.

But in pure literature we need neither exclude nor transform : experience there is *expressed* as enjoyable merely by virtue of being expressed. It is the effect of the author's intentional art both that we have the experience and that we enjoy it. This is what we mean when we say that the matter of such literature is pure experience. We may illustrate it further by contrasting Darwin with Lucretius. Both Darwin and Lucretius give us elaborate argument embodied in a mass of facts, inviting us to accept the argument as reasonable and the facts as true. Darwin's mode of expression gives us nothing else : it is expression designed to serve a purely scientific purpose, and is literature only in so far as the expression can be judged as such, taking its purpose for granted. The art of literature is not concerned with the theory of natural selection ; it is only concerned with the art which puts that theory before us. This we call applied literature ; but the poem of Lucretius we call pure literature. Why ? Because Lucretius expresses not merely a theory, but the experience of theorizing. His language certainly puts us in possession of his arguments and his facts ; but it also puts us in possession of the ardour and exultation with which he works his arguments out, the relish with which he seizes on his facts. Whether his doctrine convinces us or not, we enter, as we read him, not merely into philosophy, but also into the experience of being a philosopher, the sublime experience (to which intellect, emotion, and sense all contribute) of encountering things with an understanding that feels itself equal to them.

This brings us to a most important principle in the theory of literature ; indeed, out of the apparently simple proposition that literature expresses pure experience, all the main principles of our theory proceed. And first comes this : the importance of combining the ideas of expression and representation in the larger and livelier idea of communication. The author, at his end, expresses an experience

Cc   33

in language ; to the reader, at the other end, language represents an experience. Neither of these terms fully declares what literature is. For literature *communicates* experience : that is to say, the experience which lived in the author's mind must live again in the reader's mind. It is not enough to give the reader *what* has been experienced ; neither is it enough to give him *how* the experience has been taken. The experience itself must be given, transplanted from one mind to another. I do not give you my experience of looking at a landscape if my words merely represent what I have seen, nor if they merely express my feelings : if this experience is to be matter for literature, it must be the experience whole and entire, both what I saw and what I felt in perfect combination.

For the matter of literature, nothing else is required ; but nothing less. Attempts have often been made to say what sort of matter is suitable for pure literature, what sort is unsuitable. Anything whatever is suitable matter for the art of literature, provided it is taken by the author as experience enjoyable for its own sake, and so given to the reader ; nothing whatever is matter for literature, unless it can be so

34

taken and so given. Anything can be so taken ; but not everything can be so given. That must depend on the author's (or would-be author's) power of making language his communication. But how can language communicate experience ? It is time to look a little more closely at this. And when we do so, we cannot but see that to speak of language communicating experience is a somewhat elliptical way of speaking : though not quite so elliptical as might at first appear. Nothing can be more privately and peculiarly one's own than one's experience : it is the very process of one's life, and by no possibility can any person share his own individual life with another person. But my life can *imitate* your experience—by imagining it ; and in the case of literature, the imitation will be of the same kind as the original. For the art of literature deals wholly with the kind of experience which is, not necessarily imaginary, but certainly imaginative. The originating impulse which prompted literary composition may derive from any of the infinite possibilities of life : it may be purely imaginary, or absolutely actual : the author may have dreamt a dream, or he may have fallen in love. But whatever it

35

was, it must have become imagination : in order to put it into words, the author must catch it out of the flux of life, and hold it distinctly before him. That is to say, he must continue its existence by making it continue in imagination.

Now, for an author to communicate this means that he must arouse a similar imagination in his readers. By means of words, he must not only set imagination working in his readers ; he must also, by his words, control his readers' imagination, so that their experience may, as closely as possible, *imitate* his own. But in order to do that, he must make these very words (in a somewhat different sense) *imitate* his experience : he must make them a *symbol* of his own experience, always governing this not only by his sense of expressing himself in the symbol, but also by his understanding of his symbol's power of representing his experience to his readers. If the language he uses does not represent his experience to his readers, no matter how clearly it expresses this to himself, it does not succeed in being literature : it does not succeed as communication.

For language, in literature, must always

be symbolic. Literature communicates experience ; but experience does not happen in language. The author's experience must be translated into such symbolic equivalence in language that the symbol may be translated back again by the reader into a similar experience : in both cases, the experience being imagined. Now this symbolic medium, language, is a limited medium. But there is no limit to the possibilities of imaginative experience. The art of literature, then, is the art of using a limited medium as the symbol of unlimited possibilities. Hence it is that the literary artist must know how to combine in his art every power he can find in language which can be both expressive and representative : whatever can be *communicative*, in the sense of simultaneously stimulating and guiding imagination. The language must be expressive, for it must be the author's own experience that is transmitted ; but it must also be language that can represent experience, for otherwise this will not arrive in the reader's mind. The business would be easy, if it were true that whatever is expressive is thereby also representative. But this is not true. An exclamation may be very expressive to the

37

man who exclaims ; but to the man who hears it, it may represent little or nothing. An author may be tempted to invent new syllables, which to him may exactly express his mind : but the invention will have nothing to do with the art of literature unless these liberties unmistakably represent his mind to his readers : which they are not very likely to do.

Nevertheless, language in literature must be made to mean very much more than the logical or grammatical meaning which is given by its syntax—the orderly arrangement of its parts. In fact, literary language differs from ordinary language precisely by the conscious and deliberate use in it of powers additional to the force of grammatical meaning : powers which are only casually employed in common speech. *Thought* is not expressed in literature for its own sake, but for the sake of the organisation it gives to experience. Not only thought, but equally emotions, sensuous impressions, psychological intuitions, and the mass of infinitely variable associations that accompany the movement of thought, must also be communicated to the reader's mind : that is to say, experience itself, by being imaginatively provoked there.

Thus, as we have already noticed, something infinitely variable (experience) must be committed to a notation (language), the capacity of which is, by its very nature, limited. Literary art, therefore, will always be in some degree *suggestion* ; and the height of literary art is to make the power of suggestion in language as commanding, as far-reaching, as vivid, as subtle as possible. This power of suggestion supplements whatever language gives merely by being plainly understood ; and what it gives in this way is by no means confined to its syntax. But for conveying the finest and, perhaps, the most individual qualities of his imagination, the author must rely on his readers' ability to respond to what his language can only suggest. Socrates derived the power of literary creation from a certain *special nature*, which he described as being capable of " enthusiasm." This is true enough ; but " enthusiasm " is of no avail without the power to express it intelligibly in words. It is the *sense of language* that distinguishes the literary artist from his fellows : and the supreme test of this is knowledge of what language can be relied on to suggest. Just so it is the sense of language, proved by ability to

39

respond to the suggestions of language, that makes the enjoyer of literary art. This is that *special nature* which, active in the creator and passive in the enjoyer, we must assume as the prime specific condition of literary art.

As the medium of literary art, the communicative power of language is of four main kinds. These, of course, are only separable in a theoretical analysis : actually, they are all inextricably involved in one another. They are all capable of being unmistakably understood, though this property belongs most obviously to the first. They are all capable of an endless range of suggestion, though this may seem peculiarly noticeable in the other three. Language consists of the meaning of words and of the sound of words. These are the two aspects of one essentially indivisible combination ; but each aspect can be separately attended to. And each of these can again be subdivided into two. Of the meaning of words, there is first the grammatical meaning of the sentences given by the syntax. This is the structure of language and represents thought as the structure of experience. But every individually significant word may have, independent of its grammatical force, a peculiar *value* for imagination, derived from its context. For what a word means is by no means a simple affair. The meaning which the dictionaries give is not much more than the nucleus round which clusters a whole system of secondary meanings. The nucleus of meaning stands for a certain thing or action ; the secondary meanings indicate the various ways the thing or action can occur. A very large part of literary skill consists in vividly liberating for its effect on imagination just that particular secondary meaning in words which is not only appropriate to the immediate occasion, but which will make the occasion come to life in the reader's mind.

The meaning of words is inseparably conveyed by their sound ; but in addition to this, the sound of words can be made significant on its own account. There is first *syllabic* sound—the quality of the vowels and consonants in distinct syllables, or in sequence of syllables, brought out by contrast or by repetition. This includes, besides rhyme and alliteration, those subtly significant effects by which vowels or consonants, sounding against each other, become sometimes plainly imitative, more often indefinably but irresistibly suggestive. Secondly, there is the *rhythm* of language: not the *quality* of the sounds of syllables, but the undulation of the *degree* of sounds in whole sentences. The degree may concern strength, duration, or pitch of sound ; and the undulation is rhythmical in so far as it is a recognizable alternation of any or all of these variable degrees of sound. Rhythm is, no doubt, the most valuable use in literary art of the sound of words ; since for the most part it is rhythm which conveys the emotional atmosphere, without which experience could not live.

By considering language, then, first as meaning, and secondly as sound, and by subdividing each of these aspects into language in continuity, and language in individual words, we see that the art of literature can avail itself of a fourfold power of communication : (1) in sentences of language, there are (*a*) the syntax of the sense and (*b*) the rhythm of the sound ; (2) in individual words, there are (*a*) the imaginative value of the sense and (*b*) the syllabic quality of the sound. Thus, in the line

Crossing the stripling Thames at Bablockhithe,

the meaning of the phrase as a whole is
given by the syntax, and the rhythm of it
by the alternation of unstressed and stressed
syllables ; while the imaginative value of
the word " stripling " here is unmistakable, and the quality of syllabic sound in
the sequence of consonants and vowels
in *stripling*. *Thames, Bablockhithe* is equally
noticeable and effective (the suggestion of
the sound of flowing water is obvious).

All four kinds of power need not always
be simultaneously employed, or employed
with anything like the same degree of importance. The art of literature is often
divided into prose and poetry. This is
undeniably convenient ; but the division
cannot properly be made hard and fast.
When it is so made, it is found to depend
on nothing more than the presence or ab-
sence of a particular kind of rhythm,
which we call metre. But verse (or
language disposed in metrical rhythm)
is notoriously no guarantee of poetical
language ; and poetical language (as in
the Authorized Version of the Book of Job)
can exist very well without verse : un-
metrical rhythm may often be the right
rhythm for poetical language. But without
some such definable criterion as verse,

what is poetical language shades off into what is not poetical, by quite imperceptible degrees. The distinction, then, is only valid in a very broad sense, and is practical rather than philosophical. But it would not be even practical unless " poetical language " meant something. What does it mean ? It means language which is capable of communicating the peculiar character of an author's experience with the most penetrating vigour, the finest definition, and the subtlest detail : it means language raised to the height of its power, language in which the utmost appropriate use is simultaneously made of all its four kinds of communication. It is true that, in the vast majority of cases, when the desire is to communicate exactly every instant of experience in its immediate intensity, the peculiar insistence of metrical rhythm is employed. But metrical rhythm is not the essential thing.

The word *poetry*, then, so understood, may very well stand for literature in general, in our discussion of literary art as a whole. For poetry is the essence of literature ; in poetry, the whole business of literature, the communication of pure experience in language, is concentrated to

44

its utmost intensity. Whatever is true, on
general grounds, of poetry, will be true of
literature as a whole ; and whenever our
theory speaks of poetry, it will be of poetry
as the type of the art of literature.

The end or aim of that art is to express,
to represent, to communicate. Literature
is not composed in order to be beautiful :
we judge it to be beautiful when it has
succeeded in its aim. Just as we judge the
pure experience of looking at a landscape
to be beautiful, so do we judge the pure
experience of receiving the communication
of literature : for the experience of receiving the communication and the experience
communicated are indistinguishable. But
we have not yet completed our discussion
of the art of communicating experience in
language. We may judge many things in
the texture of a poem to be beautiful ;
and we may judge the poem as a whole
to be beautiful. But the beauty of the
whole is not merely the sum of the beauty
of the parts. So far we have been account-
ing for the *matter* in a work of literature ;
we must now speak of its *form*—that which
enables us to judge the work as a whole.
We shall find that the form of literature is
just as important as its matter. It is form

45

that gives the answer to the question, What is the function of literature?

We have seen that every work of literature originates in an experience. It may be any sort of experience : something may have happened to the author in actual life, or he may have heard a story of something, or some fantasy may have flashed into his mind. But it must be an experience peculiar in one respect : it must be of a kind to take hold of him and to demand utterance. There might be nothing extraordinary in an experience that merely urged him to express himself; there must be something extraordinary in any experience that urges him to express himself to perfection, and in a way that will also represent his experience to another mind : in a word, that insists on being communicated. For this means the energetic exertion and strict discipline of effort, in order to produce in language a symbol of the experience that shall be as nearly as possible exactly right to his artistic conscience. What is his artistic conscience? Nothing but the experience itself demanding its just equivalent in language : a severe taskmaster, to which the artist willingly

46

subjects himself. And what peculiarity must the experience have, to give it this tyrannous power over the artist's mind? The answer seems to be, a peculiar degree of intensity. Perhaps all experience demands expression; but only a peculiarly intense experience demands that remarkable kind of expression which takes the form of artistic communication, seeking thereby not merely to proclaim its occurrence, but to proclaim *itself*: so to declare its very nature and substance and tone that it may come to life again in other minds.

Now, intensity of experience means intensity of attention to it. We may call an experience, which possesses this power of dominating and energizing the artist's mind, the *inspiration* of the resulting work of art: a useful word, so long as we confine it to this quite precise meaning. In this sense of the word, the rule is, that the greater the inspiration, the greater the art required to give it literary expression; for the more there is in an experience, the more power over language will be required to symbolize it in a work of art. It is plain that the writers—Homer, Dante, Shakespeare, Milton—who can give us the

47

greatest experiences, can do so because they are the writers who have the greatest command of expression in language. Of course, they had great inspiration ; but we should not know that if their language had not been adequate to it. The richer the substance of their experience, the richer they could make the texture of their poetry : but that was because of their power over language. It was not merely, however, the wealth of substance in it that made their experience an inspiration ; it was because this wealth of substance was attended to in a single intensity of experience. When Shakespeare heard (or read) the story of *Othello*, he took it as a single experience ; the whole matter and import of the tale was seized by him in a single act of imaginative attention. The wealth of matter in this experience of his is expressed by the texture of the play ; but the final impression of the completed play brings all this wealth of matter in our minds into a single intensity of experience, a single act of imaginative attention, the excitement of which corresponds (so far as we are able to correspond) with the energy of Shakespeare's inspiration.

Experience can never be simple. It must always at least unite what is given to a mind with what is given by the mind ; and both of these may be complicated. Suppose a man is looking at a sunset. His senses do not only give him the glory of colour and the delight of shape ; they also give him, perhaps, the coolness, the quiet, the fragrance of the moment. And to these he adds, perhaps, imaginative associations of his own : all that the appearance of fire means to him, all that is suggested by the end of day, the coming of night, the transitoriness of beauty, and so on. All this is united in a single experience ; all this is collected in a single act of attention. If the moment has the intensity which demands artistic expression, it will be picked out of the flux of experience, isolated, and made to persist by being continued in imagination ; and by the very act of being imagined, it will be still more enriched. Now what characterizes this experience is not merely the substance of which it is composed, but the unity in which this complex substance is held by imaginative attention. And if this experience is to be communicated *as such*, not only must literature symbolize its

Dc
49

complex substance, it must also symbolize the peculiar unity in which that substance has been held by the author's imaginative attention : the very unity, in fact, which made it his inspiration.

That aspect of literature which symbolizes the substance of the originating experience we may call its *diction* ; the aspect which symbolizes the unity of the substance in a single act of comprehensive attention we call the *form* of a piece of literature. Form is not imposed on diction by some sort of external application ; form arises out of diction, when the diction truly corresponds with its inspiration. Nevertheless form in literature is an aspect of it as distinguishable from diction as the meaning of language is distinguishable from its sound : and it is important both in theory and in criticism that the distinction should be made.

Since experience cannot be directly transferred from one mind to another, but can only be communicated by a symbol, and since in literature the symbol consists of words and combinations of words which are successively put together and successively understood, it follows that the first thing to do in communicating an

inspiration is to disintegrate its unity into
the parts of which it was composed, and
that the first thing to happen in receiving
an inspiration must be to take in the parts
of it piecemeal. But the artist in thus
putting forth his inspiration must provide,
all the time he is doing so, for the reintegration of its parts once more into
a unity, when the process of their succession is finally complete ; so that the
mind that receives his art will have re-
ceived a series of impressions in a certain
shapeliness of succession that will give, at
the moment when the series is complete,
a *form* to the mass of his experiences,
whereby all the successive impressions
unite in a single organic whole.

Of form in literature, thus considered as
the symbolic equivalent of the characteristic unity of inspiration (as diction is the
equivalent of its characteristic substance),
the importance appears when we ask,
What is the function of literature ? To
what end is this communicating of pure
experience in plays, poems, and novels ?
What do we gain thereby, if we do not
gain information, nor persuasion of the
truth, the moral worth, the utility of
things ? It might seem a sufficient answer

simply to say, that we gain experience ; and since it is *by* experience, and primarily *in* experience, that we live at all, to gain experience simply as such is a gain in being alive. But this would put literature in competition with actual life ; and literature can never compete with actual life in the mere provision of experience ; for literature can never be anything but imagined experience, which, in competition with actuality, is always under the grave disadvantage of, precisely, not being actual. It is when we look to the form of literature that we see the remarkable advantage over actuality in the experience which literature can provide. For it is the nature of man never to be satisfied with himself simply as the being that experiences ; the whole of his practical and speculative effort is to make, or to discover, significance in his experience. Now, in literature, we do not need to make, or to discover, significance in our experience there ; experience there *is* significant, simply by virtue of being literature.

And that by reason of the *form* which literature gives to experience. Our practical and speculative efforts are always to advance towards the perfect significance

52

of life as organized fact, or philosophic truth, or moral value, or convenient utility ; but they never arrive, and they never will arrive. There is no advance in literature. If literature succeeds in coming into existence, the experience it gives us is thereby significant : it was so when first it was composed, and will be so for ever. If the experience is not significant, literature has not succeeded in coming into existence.

For what is this most fundamental of all man's desires, the desire that his experience should be significant ? It cannot be, that experience should have a meaning outside itself : what meaning intelligible to us could experience have outside itself— to us who cannot pass beyond our experience ? It can only be, that experience should have a meaning within itself. But what do we mean by " meaning " ? Simply, the inevitable relation which one thing has with another. A thing is said to be full of meaning, when it is a focus of relationship with many other things. Experience is perfectly significant, when everything in it is a focus of relationships with everything else in it. It is our nature to detest that kind of experience in which things are incoherent, and happen (or

53

seem to happen) independent of the rest of things—or, as we say, *by chance*. Significant experience is experience in which nothing happens by chance, but everything happens in complete coherence with the rest : everything there exists not only for its own sake, but also for the sake of the whole : the whole is implied by the manner in which everything occurs in it. Each part is more than itself ; for it *means* more than itself—it means the furtherance of the organizing of a whole manifestly ordained.

Now this is exactly what experience is in literature. In a work of literature—poem, play, novel, essay, or whatever it may be, so long as it truly is literature—nothing happens that does not somehow contribute to the form of the work as a whole, to the finally unified impression of all the sequence of impressions it has given us. This is, certainly, a limited experience, for it corresponds with that experience which the author's imaginative attention seized on and isolated out of the flux of things, and maintained as an inspiration. But precisely, of course, because it is so limited has this experience the unity which gives it significance. Now it is possible that many people, who have not the literary artist's power of expression, may nevertheless have moments of experience of a nature similar to his. But in literature we can all have them whenever we want. Moreover—and this is the important point—in literature the significance is given to us in a way that makes it much more noticeable than if it came in an instantaneous intuition of actual things. The literary artist has to build up in his symbolic medium, gradually and deliberately, the organic unity of his work. Hence, when we live in a work of literature, we live in a series of impressions, every one of which we feel is contributing to the final impression of the *form* of the work as a completed whole. We live in experience which we know is ordained to be, however complex, at last a unity. When we have the form of the work as a whole in our minds, we have the unity of all the experience it has given us ; and having the unity, we have our experience organized in perfect interrelationship ; we have what the whole manner of the work has made us expect and desire : we have, on a greater or lesser scale, experience that is completely significant. This is the kind of experience we are always hoping for ;

but only in art do we get it : not merely a flashing accidental moment of unified experience, but a prolonged continuous series of moments securely and infallibly organizing their own perfect system of interrelationship, and thereby manifesting the only significance which is absolutely necessary to our minds—the revelation of law and order in things. The enemy of this is chance ; only in art are we safe from the enemy.

Here, then, is the function of literature ; and to find it we have not gone beyond the sphere of literature, *pure experience*, judged simply for what it is in itself. To say that the function of literature is to teach us or convince us or make us moral is to step outside the literary art. Literature can do these things, but it is not by virtue of doing them that it is literature. Neither is it the function of literature to be beautiful ; we should rather say, one of the things we may judge to be beautiful in literature is the way it achieves its function. That function is, by its expression of experience as such, to make experience significant as such without our having to judge it as true or real or useful or moral. Every work of literature, though the

56

experience it gives us is necessarily limited, provides us with an instance of the experience we most profoundly need : and that by reason of its form. It is form in literature that makes experience there significant. But it is obviously incorrect, though it may be convenient, to speak of significant form. Form itself cannot be significant. Form can only exist as the form of substance ; and the significance given by form is significance which form gives to substance. That substance, it is true, is not actual substance. But in actual experience, we can never know complete and secure significance. If we wish to know what that is, we must be content with imagined experience. But the perfect significance we find in the imagined life of literature is a continual incentive to the noblest endeavour of actual life : the endeavour to attain, practically or intellectually, as much significance as may be.

It will be useful to conclude this section by recapitulating in a tabular summary the main principles of the theory of the art of literature.

1. The art of literature is the art of communicating in language experience valued as such and enjoyable for its own sake.

2. For this, it is not enough to communicate either the matter or the manner of the experience : it is not enough to express the subject of the experience, nor to represent the object of the experience : it is the experience itself, whole and entire, both the object and the subject, the thing that happened and the mind to which it happened, that must be communicated.

3. Since the experience did not happen in language, language can only communicate it symbolically ; the power of language to symbolize experience depending on its power to stimulate imagination. Whatever the experience may have originally been, it must always be communicated as imagination.

4. In order to symbolize experience as completely as possible—that is, to provoke the most complex imagination possible—literature makes appropriate use of every power language has of affecting the mind, both on the semantic side (or the aspect of meaning) and on the phonetic side (or the aspect of the sound of language). The power of language over the mind is fourfold :

58

Semantic : the construction of the meaning in syntax, and the imaginative value of individual words ;

Phonetic : the construction of the sound in rhythm, and the quality of individual syllables.

5. An experience is characterized not only by its substance, but also by the unity in which its substance is held. To communicate an experience is therefore to communicate both its substance and its unity. The diction of literature symbolizes the substance of the experience inspiring it, the form of literature symbolizes the unity of this. In order to commit experience to the communication of language, it must be disintegrated ; but as the communication progresses, there must be a governing tendency towards a final reintegration into unity. So that as the series of impressions goes on, the diction designs itself as form ; and when the diction is complete, the form is achieved.

6. When the whole series of impressions can be seen as constituting a single shapely form, and therefore as a unity, everything in a work of literature is understood as existing in perfect interrelationship. Nothing

59

is there by chance ; nothing is there unless in the interest of the whole. This is
that significance in experience which we
desire above all things. To provide us with
vivid imagination of significant experience
is the function of literature.

III. ARISTOTLE'S "POETICS"

III. ARISTOTLE'S "POETICS"

ARISTOTLE'S treatise *Concerning the Art of Poetry,* usually called the *Poetics,*[1] was never meant by Aristotle himself to be a treatise. Like almost everything else of his that has survived, it was not composed as a book ; it merely represents the lectures which he used to give his students. It may be the notes which he himself set down for his own guidance ; it may be the notes which some student or students took of his lectures ; it may be a mixture of both. Whoever committed it to writing did not do so for the public to read. It is abrupt, disjointed, awkwardly terse, as awkwardly digressive ; essential ideas are left unexplained, inessential things are elaborated. In short, it has all the literary defects of lecture notes. The most important conception in it, the intellectual centre round which everything else is organized, is never defined ; it is mentioned by a technical term (which is not only metaphorical, but

[1] Good English translations are Butcher's (Macmillan's) and Bywater's (Clarendon Press).

ambiguously metaphorical) and is fre-
quently alluded to ; but we have to make
out, as best we may, what Aristotle means
by it. This is exactly what one might expect of lecture notes. The central idea of his
system was precisely that which least of all
needed to be written out in full : precisely
that on which he could trust himself to
lecture without notes.

In spite of all these defects, the argument majestically reveals itself : and the
argument is such, that the *Poetics* is not
only the first thoroughly philosophical
discussion of literature, but the foundation
of all subsequent discussions. It is, of
course, the product of its time ; a fact
which is most obviously apparent in the
limitation of its subject matter ; for literature has developed in many directions
since Aristotle's time. It is fatally easy for
criticism to go wrong, when it is restricted,
or restricts itself, to a few kinds and fash-
ions in literature : it is fatally easy to take
the inessential for the essential. But Aristotle had the conscience of a philosopher.
With him, discussion of the problems of
literary criticism, however restricted in
scope, could not but be a truly philosophical discussion. What was good

philosophy in Greece in the fourth century before Christ, is good philosophy everywhere and in every age. Much of what he says illustrates Greek thought and concerns Greek literature ; but much of what he says is the essence of right thinking about literature in general. In many respects, nothing has been added, and so far as one can see, nothing ever will be added, to what Aristotle had to say about the art of literature. Thus, though it must always be important to consider the *Poetics* as belonging to Greek culture, for us the important thing is to consider the book simply as an exposition of the principles of literary criticism, as valid for Shakespeare and Milton as for Homer and Sophocles. Nothing could be more misleading than to attribute to Aristotle modern ways of thought and feeling ; nothing could be more illuminating than to test his principles by applying them to modern expressions of thought and feeling.

The subject matter of the *Poetics*, as the book has come down to us, is not merely restricted to Greek literature, but to certain kinds of Greek literature. These are four in number ; and Aristotle groups them in pairs, according to their historical and æsthetic connexions. He supposes poetry to begin in two kinds, as the originating motive of all poetry tended, by its very nature, to diverge in two directions. Poetry, namely, begins either as heroic or as satiric poetry : but out of heroic (or epic) poetry develops tragedy, out of satiric comes comedy. Since, then, the nature of poetry thus disposes itself into two pairs of kinds, the principles valid for epic will, with the proper modification, be valid also for tragedy, those valid for satire will be similarly valid for comedy. But Aristotle regarded the historically later kind in each pair as a higher development of poetic art, and as therefore requiring fuller discussion than the earlier kind. Accordingly his scheme is to work out the theory of the later development and then, adapting it to different but closely related conditions, to apply it to the earlier kind. But the *Poetics*, as we have the book, is not complete. The scheme of the discussion is unmistakably indicated ; but actually we are only given the discussion of tragedy, and the application of its results to epic poetry. There can be no doubt that the original treatise contained a second

part, now lost, in which comedy and satire
were similarly treated.

· Broadly taken, this scheme of Aristotle's
is sound enough. But it must always be
remembered that the division of poetry
(or literature in general) into kinds or
species, though the demarcation may be
sometimes very obvious, is in the last re-
sort only commendable as a convenience
of discussion. It is not like the division of
animals into species : there are no biological boundaries in poetry. Aristotle
sometimes forgets that to condemn a composition as a tragedy is not necessarily to
condemn it as a poem. It may have
seemed, by certain apparent signs, to resemble tragedy ; but the real purpose may
have been something quite different. It is
also possible that the species " tragedy "
may have been too rigidly defined. But
what is more likely to strike a modern
reader, in this scheme of Aristotle's, is its
complete omission of lyric poetry. This is
not likely to be due to inadvertence.
Neither is the cause of this likely to have
been, that lyric poetry would not fall in
well with the sort of argument to which
Aristotle's philosophical tendencies inclined. On the contrary, lyric poetry

would have given him invaluable aid in making out his central proposition. The thing probably was, that for Aristotle lyric poetry was inseparably bound up with music; just as for most of us to-day " Drink to me only with thine eyes " or " Auld lang syne " only exists as a poem in conjunction with its melody. Lyric poetry would therefore scarcely fall within the scope of his topic ; for he expressly limits the art of poetry to the medium of language. What we have, then, in Aristotle's *Poetics*, is really the theory of tragedy, with the modification of this to cover epic. But the theory of tragedy is worked out with such insight and comprehension, that it becomes the type of the theory of literature.

To a philosopher like Aristotle, whose ambition seems to have been to systematize the whole range of man's mental activity, it would scarcely have been possible to omit so conspicuous a part of it as the art of literature. But almost certainly his argument had another, and perhaps a more keenly urgent motive than that ; almost certainly the *Poetics* is Aristotle's counterblast to Plato's celebrated condemnation of poetry as a pursuit unworthy of man's intellectual dignity, and radically vicious in its effect. In introducing the *Poetics*, therefore, something must be said, however briefly and inadequately, about the difference between these two typical minds ; for, as far as our topic is concerned, out of this difference came the most formidable assault on poetry, and the most effective defence of it, that has ever been known.

Aristotle had been Plato's pupil ; but as his mind matured, he became conscious of a deep cleavage between his convictions and his master's, and felt himself called upon to protest against some of the characteristic conclusions and methods of the Platonic philosophy. Indeed, it would scarcely be possible to pick out two men better fitted to illustrate the two opposite poles of philosophic thinking. The difference between the two may, very roughly, be indicated by referring to the studies in which they were specially interested. Aristotle's philosophy was coloured by his interest in biology, Plato's by his interest in mathematics. This means that Aristotle's mind liked to proceed from things to ideas, Plato's from ideas to things. Aristotle had the scientific, Plato the metaphysical mind. The great importance of this difference between them comes in when the question is, What is meant by *reality* ? Thus, the biologist may be led by the study of actual individual creatures to the general idea of a species of creatures, Man or Dog. The idea of a species is real enough ; but it is real only because it is the idea of real men and dogs. Biologically speaking, the reality of things gives to ideas whatever reality they possess. But mathematically speaking, the reality of ideas gives to things whatever reality they possess. For the mathematician studies ideas which cannot be perfectly realized in things. The idea of a line is purely an idea, and the properties of a line are purely ideal properties. But they are eternal and immutable properties, in which the mind may rest with absolute conviction. In a word, they are the properties of that certainty of existence we call reality ; and actual physical lines only possess these properties in so far as they are able to represent the idea of a line, which they can only do approximately. Thus for the mathematical mind things are real enough but only because they represent ideas ; reality is conferred on things by ideas ; the ideas would be real even if (as in fact is the case with many mathematical ideas) there were no things to represent them.

This digression may seem to have moved a long way from poetry. By what perverse logic Plato arrived at his condemnation of poetry, we shall presently see ; but the nature of his objection is quite in accordance with the nature of his philosophy, just as Aristotle's answer to that objection accords with the nature of *his* philosophy, and with his antipathy to Plato's. Aristotle never says that his theory is an answer to Plato ; he never mentions Plato in the *Poetics*, and never even alludes to the Platonic objection to poetry. But his whole argument is exactly planned to invalidate Plato's argument at every point ; and thus falls in with his openly expressed opposition to Plato elsewhere. The difference between the two minds is shown in the way they approach the very existence of poetry. It seems a paradox that Plato, who in his youth had done exquisite things in poetry, and in his maturity had such perfect command of literary art that he could present abstrusest metaphysics as an enchanting music of ideas, should have been the man to condemn poetry ; whereas

71

Aristotle, whose extant works can scarcely be called literature at all, should have directed the full force of his philosophy into the sanest and strongest commendation poetry has ever had. But we must remember that Aristotle is not to be judged as a writer by his extant works; the books by which he might have been so judged have almost entirely disappeared. Nevertheless, it seems unlikely that Aristotle could ever have stood beside Plato as a literary artist. But it was Plato the philosopher who condemned poetry; and the mere fact that he did so is typical of the way his philosophy regarded *things*. Things being only important as the representatives of ideas, he was quite prepared to say that a thing which was unnecessary or unworthy as a representative of ideas ought not to exist. Poetry was a thing of this nature; Plato therefore proposed that it should be abolished. But it was with a biologist's respect for the existence of *things* that Aristotle looked on poetry : for him, ideas were only important as the interpretation of things. It never occurs to Aristotle to ask whether poetry ought or ought not to exist. It does exist: the questions for *his* philosophy are, In what

manner and to what result does it exist ?
One might perhaps say, Aristotle would no
more think of asking whether poetry ought
to exist, than whether a species of animals
ought to exist. At any rate, the conclusion
he comes to is the exact opposite of
Plato's opinion ; it is, that the function
of poetry can be supremely beneficent.
It may very well be that he started with
this opinion ; and that to prove it against
the great authority of Plato was his chief
motive in composing the *Poetics*. The
thing is, that his argument arrives at this
conclusion by a strictly philosophical
process. Aristotle's philosophical conscience ensures that the result would be the
same, whether the investigation did or did
not begin as a perfectly disinterested en-
terprise.

But no systematic philosopher can be
perfectly disinterested when he investi-
gates a special topic ; he has, at least, the
interests of his system in his mind—if he
had not, it would not be a system with any
life in it. Aristotle's philosophy was mag-
nificently systematic ; and it was vividly
alive. Its characteristic habit of life is
apparent throughout the *Poetics*. We find
there methods and notions that are

sometimes more appropriate to Aristotle than to the subject. An invaluable method in biological research is classification. The *Poetics* is full of it. When he is defining his topic, Aristotle's mastery of this difficult method does noble service ; but afterwards, in the exposition of the topic, he sometimes classifies where no classification is needed, sometimes where no classification can be valid, sometimes where any classification must be misleading. We shall pay no attention to all this, since for us it is not his methods, but his results that matter. Again, the ethical notion of " the golden mean," so dear to Aristotle, insinuates itself into the argument in a manner which cannot be so persuasive to us as it evidently was to him.

But often his philosophical habits are most admirable when they seem to appear most casually. Thus, in the very first sentence of the treatise, he completely disposes of the theory of " Art for Art's sake " simply by describing his subject in terms satisfactory to a biological philosopher. " I shall speak," he says, " of the art of poetry and of its various species, discussing the function of each kind, along with the proper structure of a poem and

74

the number and nature of its parts." It would be easy to pass over this sentence as a mere formal introduction ; but every clause of it is important. It posits the whole subject with truly scientific comprehension. To know what poetry really is, we must know not only its anatomy and physiology ; we must know its natural history also. We do not know what an animal truly is, until we have not only dissected it, but also have accurately observed how it behaves. The nature of animal life, the species of the animal, the structure of its body, the number and nature of its organs : we may know all this, but what the animal truly *is* will escape us, unless we also know what it can *do*, how it comports itself, in its natural surroundings. So it is with poetry. Poetry is one of the activities of human nature : but exactly what this activity is we shall never know unless, besides analysing it, we note what it effects among the other activities of human nature : unless, that is to say, we note the *function* of poetry. Poetry must have some function : for, in the world of human activity, it must somehow *behave* : all human activities take place in human nature, and must therefore affect each other. Now, if the phrase " Art for Art's sake " means that art can never be understood, if we judge it according to something outside the nature of art, the phrase is a very salutary warning. But if it means, as it nearly always does, that art has no function in life, then the manifest falsity of the phrase is at once shown up simply by formulating what it is we require to know in order to understand what art truly is. As Aristotle's introductory sentence indicates, æsthetic investigation is exactly analogous with biological investigation. To know what poetry *is*, we must not only examine its organism : we must know what this organism can *do* in its natural habitat—the lives of human beings. We must know its function. But its function will be conditioned by the nature of its structure, and the parts out of which its whole structure is made.

Aristotle begins his investigation by calling poetry a mode of " imitation." This was in accordance with the Greek habit of thinking about all " fine art," just as it accords with our way of thinking to call art a mode of " expression." As casually as we talk of expression, the Greeks talked of imitation ; and neither

term is very helpful unless it is defined.
We must remember that the Greek word
for art never acquired that limitation of
meaning which our word has in the phrase
" fine art." For the Greek mind, activity
was either doing things or making things.
In doing things, the action itself was to be
judged ; in making things, the action was
to be judged by what it made—the tan-
gible object which it brought into existence. It was in the latter case that activity was an art. The value of the art was
easily judged, when the thing it produced
was a shoe or a pot. But how if the thing
produced was a picture or a poem ? In
that case, the value of the thing did not
consist in its material, nor even in the arrangement of its material : it consisted in
the way the material and its arrangement
stood for something. The Greeks said, it
consisted in the way the product imitated
something.

So far, the word is completely vague :
but it was as imitation that the Greek
mind naturally explained the existence of
what we call art (meaning " fine art ") ;
and Aristotle inevitably made this ele-
mentary notion the starting point of his
theory. The originality of his theory

consists in the direction its argument took
from this notion. The easy and obviously
inviting way to argue from it would be
to say that art imitates nature : art, then,
is the skilled copying or mimicry of the
objects we know in the world. This was
the popular way of arguing ; and it was
also Plato's way. It enabled him, in conjunction with his *theory of ideas* (which,
however, he had to strain somewhat for
the purpose) to give a plausibly reasoned
form to his disparagement of poetry—indeed, of art in general. The accusation he
brought against poetry was as complete
as it could be ; the nature of poetry, he
said, was wholly unworthy of serious attention, the function of poetry was radically vicious. This latter charge will be
described later ; at present, we are concerned with his attack on the nature of
poetry—on poetry, namely, as *imitation.*
Aristotle, too, in the early part of his
treatise, was no doubt concerned with
Plato's attack on the imitative nature of
poetry ; and he meets the accusation of
consequent unworthiness by giving a
completely different interpretation of the
whole notion of imitation in poetry.
Aristotle's way of interpreting poetic

imitation is possibly the most valuable of all
his contributions to æsthetic theory. At
any rate, it puts the theory on perfectly
secure and solid foundations.

All the " fine arts " are connected. It
suited the tactics of Plato's attack on the
art of poetry to approach it through the art
of painting ; for the notion that imitation
is mimicry is most easily supported in
painting. The attack went thus. The only
business worthy of man's mind is his
concern with reality. Men should be concerned with *things* for their reality ; and
their reality is given to them by the ideas
they represent. Now a painter imitates
things ; and things represent ideas ; and
ideas *are* reality. Painting, therefore, only
deals with reality at third hand. Thus, in
the famous example, there are many beds
in the world ; but beds only exist because
the idea of a bed exists. When a carpenter
makes a bed, he may be said to copy the
one original and universal bed, the ideal
bed which (Plato's theory does not shrink
from this) was created by God : by which
he means, of course, that the ideal is the
only truly real. The carpenter's is a necessary and entirely worthy occupation. And
now along comes the painter, and copies

79

the bed which the carpenter made : that is to say, he copies the copy of the real bed : an unnecessary and entirely unworthy occupation. And as it is with painters, so it is with poets (Plato, like Aristotle, is thinking chiefly of epic and dramatic poets). The painter copies objects, the poet copies the behaviour of men and women : both artists copy appearances in the world of things, and their work is therefore twice removed from reality.

This abstract does not, of course, do justice to the humour, gusto, good-nature, and persuasiveness with which Plato's inimitable art conducts the argument ; but it may serve to show the strain which the argument puts on the theory of ideas. And yet, if we grant that that theory may include particular objects (and even artifacts, such as beds), and if we grant that imitation in art means mimicry, the logic is sound enough. The attack, at any rate, is not one that can be ignored ; and we must remember that Plato's attack on the nature of poetry prepared the way for a weightier assault on its function. How then is this first assault to be met ? Aristotle, in the *Poetics*, leaves the theory of ideas alone ; for it can do nothing here without the theory that poetry imitates nature, in the sense of mimicry. It will suffice to show that poetry does not imitate nature. And to show this Aristotle does not appeal to *a priori* notions ; he appeals, as a good naturalist will always do, to the facts. He does not do this directly, however ; the facts of the case are implied by the nature of his argument. But they are obvious enough. It may seem easy and inviting theory to say that art is the mirror of nature ; but since we can see nature herself, what do we want with a mirror ? If poetry merely mirrored nature, it could give us no more than nature gives us ; but the fact is, that we enjoy poetry precisely because it gives us something which nature does not give us. We may say, for example, that the persons in dramatic poetry are " like life " ; but where in actual life shall we find such persons—persons who are interesting in everything they do or say, persons who continually and inevitably reveal both themselves and the events in which they live ? The figures of such persons do not imitate nature ; and this is typical of poetry in general. What then does poetry imitate ?—But we had better follow Aristotle's argument.

Poetry, he begins, is a mode of imitation. But instead of saying, as Plato does, that in this respect it is like painting, Aristotle says that it is like music or dancing. This is significant ; for painting suggests (though quite falsely) imitation in the sense of mimicry. But the mention of music and dancing is a preliminary warning, that whatever imitation in poetry may mean, it does not mean mimicry. For what mimicry is there in music ? And, though dancing may represent passion and action, its formal rhythms and deliberate graces certainly do not copy natural gesture and movement. Aristotle then proceeds, by means of a threefold classification, to narrow down the general notion of imitation to the particular topics of his treatise. He asks, in effect, three questions : In what does the imitation exist ? What does it imitate ? How does it imitate ? That is, he classifies imitation according to its *medium*, its *object*, and its *manner*.

The *medium* of the kind of imitation with which he is concerned is, of course, language. And here he makes a remarkable reflection. He notes that the art he is to discuss has, as regards its medium, properly speaking no name—no name, at least, comparable for exact and generally agreed meaning with such names as "sculpture" or "music." And this is still true to-day. For purposes of discussion, we may use the word "poetry" for the pure art of literature. But, says Aristotle, people connect the idea of poetry with a particular kind of rhythm in language. Yet the nature of poetry is not given by metrical rhythm. Compositions which are designed to instruct or inform may be written in metre ; but they are not therefore poetry : in his terminology, they do not *imitate* anything. On the other hand, compositions may be very successful imitations (to us, "representations" would sound more familiarly) without being written in metre. The contrast, then, is not between poetry and prose ; for this simply marks a difference in technique ; the true contrast is between literature which " imitates " and that which does not ; and *either* of these two classes may be written in metrical or in non-metrical language. Thus Aristotle is the first critic to point out that the essential nature of poetry may often be found in prose ; and on the contrary, that verse is no guarantee of poetry. This short digression indicates that in the sequel his discussion of a particular kind of poetry is a type of the theory of pure literature in general.

Having thus limited his topic to what, for want of a more specific term, we must call pure literature, he goes on to classify this with respect to the *object* of the imitation. In general, he says, the object of poetic imitation is *men in action* ; which, remembering his exclusion of lyrical poetry, will be found an adequate description. For by *men in action* he does not necessarily mean *men doing things* ; he means *things happening in terms of human nature, events embodied in human lives.* In a word, he means a *story*, in the widest possible sense ; and the essential element in a story is the human element. The objects of poetic imitation, then, may be classified according to the nature of the human element in them ; and we judge human nature by its goodness or badness. Poetry, then, may represent men as better than in real life, as worse, or as they are. This third variant Aristotle merely mentions, and then ignores ; he is wholly concerned with the other two. The poetry he is to discuss imitates men either as being better than in real life, or as being worse. The purpose of

84

this classification is to derive from one common impulse the two main kinds of non-lyrical poetry, tragic and comic ; and as such it may be provisionally allowed. There is a sense in which a tragic character is better than real life, and a comic character worse. Real people do not exemplify in such capital fashion the qualities which make human nature admirable, nor those which make it ridiculous. Yet this rough sort of classification involves serious difficulties. Tragic characters are not necessarily *morally* better than in real life : witness Macbeth. But if they are said to be better in the sense of being more imposing and remarkable, may not the same thing be said of comic characters also ? Witness Falstaff.

But one thing remains quite unquestionable in this second classification of Aristotle's : poetic imitation does not mean mimicry. How can poetry imitate men as better or as worse than real life ? Obviously, not by copying nature ; but only by imitating imagination. The theoretical possibility that poetry *might* represent men " as they are," Aristotle, we have seen, mentions only to ignore ; no doubt because he did not think it worth discussing.

85

For this possibility is not characteristic of poetry. This is not what we demand of poetry ; and therefore, as a matter of practical fact, this is not what poetry does. We do not want a transcription from nature, since we have the original always before us ; we want an imaginative reconstruction of the possibilities of nature.

Plato took imitation to be the connexion between poetry and nature ; which leaves quite unexplained the characteristic quality and energy of poetry (whether in verse or in prose, whether an epic or a novel). Aristotle, with far finer discrimination, saw that the connexion effected by imitation is not between poetry and the world without, but falls wholly within the being of poetry. Poetry is not connected with the outside world in the simple and direct fashion supposed by Plato. The poet first derives an inspiration from the world by the power of his imagination ; the art of poetry then imitates this imaginative inspiration in language. Aristotle's theory is not really concerned with the nature of the originating connexion between poetry and the world, except by certain plain implications in the argument throughout, and for one anomalous digression to be noted presently. His discussion is " concerning the art of poetry." The art exists to give shape and substance to a certain kind of imaginative impulse : the existence of the art implies the existence of the impulse. Aristotle, in discussing the art, assumes the existence of the impulse ; his business is to discuss its nature, and the way it works itself out into language. But to enquire into the connexion between poetry and the world is to enquire into the origin of this impulse ; and the questions how and why it arose belong rather to psychology than to æsthetics. Now it is just possible to imagine life exactly as it is ; but the exciting thing is to imagine life as it might be, and it is then that imagination becomes an impulse capable of inspiring poetry. This is true even in the case of what we call realism in literature ; it is true even when the life imagined was originally an actuality of some highly exciting nature in itself. Imagination may do no more than concentrate the actuality, by dropping out all its insignificant passages. But that will be enough to make the resultant poetry (or literature) something quite different from that copy of the world

87

which Plato's condemnation assumed it to be.

Thus, what Aristotle means by " imitation " in poetry is exactly what we mean by *technique*. Poetic imitation, as Aristotle uses the word everywhere in his theory (with the exception of an unimportant chapter which really forms no part of his theory), does not explain the origin of poetry, nor what the connexion is between poetry and real things and affairs. Aristotle's " imitation " is confined entirely to the poetic activity within the art itself : it describes the connexion between poetic impulse and poetic language. It is his word for the technique by which the poet finally achieves communicable expression of his imaginative inspiration. We say " finally achieves " : for, whether the word be " technique " or " imitation," more is involved than the mere management of language, as we shall soon see.

It remains, in the third place, to classify works of literature according to their *manner*. There is no difficulty here. Within the scope Aristotle has assigned to his subject, all poems may be classified either as narrative or as dramatic. Thus poems which resemble each other in the object may differ in the manner of imitation, and the other way round. Sophocles as a tragic poet might be classed with Homer, but as a dramatic poet with Aristophanes.

By means of this three-fold classification, Aristotle has prepared the way for the main topic of that portion of his treatise which has survived : namely, the discussion of tragic drama. At this point, however, he (or perhaps someone else) introduces a chapter on the history and development of literature by a brief discussion of the origin of poetry. It treats this business in a feeble, perfunctory, and confused fashion, and comes to no rational conclusion. That would be no great matter, since, as we have said, Aristotle's theory is an exposition of the nature of poetry as it actually exists, and has no concern with the question, How did poetry come to exist ? What has, however, caused a good deal of misunderstanding, is the fact that, in these few sentences, the word for " imitation " is expressly used to mean " mimicry." The argument takes us nowhere ; but if it had any validity, it would make the theory in all the rest of the book wholly unintelligible. Indeed, it

would be hard to find plainer contra-
diction than that between " imitation "
everywhere else in the book, and " imitation " in this quite superfluous digression
(which merely interrupts the process of
the argument). If we wish to understand
Aristotle's theory, there is only one thing
to be done : this passage must be ignored.
We may regard it either as interpolation,
or as a queer aberration. But perhaps not
an unaccountable aberration. With Aristotle, æsthetic science first begins : it is
marvellous that it should have begun
with a treatment so precise and accurate,
that in many respects it stands as the last
as well as the first word on the subject.
But very often, when a science first distinctly emerges, it uses terms, hitherto in
vague and general use, which it has not
yet strictly defined. It is very possible that
Aristotle never consciously defined " imitation " in the sense which we have been
attributing to him. The word and the idea
were there, ready for use in discussion of
this sort ; and he used them as seemed
good to him. But his astonishingly keen
critical insight into the nature of poetry
led him to make just that specific use of
" imitation " in his theory, which is the

only intelligible use of the word and the idea in connexion with poetry : which is also, since it enabled him to discriminate between technique and inspiration, a contribution of incalculable value to the theory of literature. And though he does not define it, we are bound to attribute this specific meaning to the word " imitation " in his theory, simply because this is the only thing the word can mean as he uses it. But when he stepped for a moment outside his theory and digressed into the question of psychological origins, a quite different topic, he unconsciously allowed the word to relapse back again into its old meaning.

Coming now to his main subject of tragic poetry, and briefly noting some of the differences consequent on the different manners of epic and dramatic form, Aristotle makes a remark which has had more fame than it deserves. One very obvious difference between epic and drama is, that an epic is much longer than a drama. The reason is simple : a drama must be given complete in a single performance, but an epic is composed under no such necessity. This naturally involves a difference in content ; but for Aristotle, with only the practice of Greek drama before him, the difference in content presented itself in a very noticeable way. Drama, he says, tends, " as far as possible," to confine its action to twenty-four hours, whereas epic action need have no limitation in respect of time. This casual remark simply refers to the practice of Greek tragedy, not to anything inherent in the nature of drama. Owing to its peculiar origin and circumstances, Greek tragedy presented its story in an unbroken continuity of action. The sort of story that would best fit in with this mode of dramatic presentation was evidently one that implied no great break in the time, and no great change in the place, of its occurrence. This was a mere matter of practical convenience. But since the tragic chorus might from time to time hold the movement of the story suspended in lyrical comment on it, the dramatist had the opportunity of introducing supposed intervals of time, as well as supposed changes of place, if it suited his story to do so. The Greek tragic poets made no difficulty about occasionally availing themselves of this opportunity. Aristotle himself admits that the rule was not absolute as regards time ; about place he says nothing.

Intrinsically, the remark that tragedy " endeavours, as far as possible, to confine itself to the events of twenty-four hours," is of small importance. It is a good instance of the way Aristotle's illustration of his theory was limited by the literature of his time ; it is also a good instance of the way he refused to dogmatize on purely accidental qualities. But in the history of criticism, this remark is of immense importance : an importance given to it by the power of sheer misunderstanding. Everyone has heard of the dogma of the Three Unities in drama—unity of action, unity of time, unity of place. Had it not been for this casual remark of Aristotle's, the dogma would never have been formulated. But Aristotle cannot be held responsible for conclusions which merely mistake his meaning. Critics, from the Renaissance onwards, especially in France and Italy, dogmatically maintained the Three Unities as the great principle of dramatic composition, appealing to the example of the Greek tragedians and the authority of Aristotle. Now, for unity of action, which simply means that a poem must be a single

93

organic whole, Greek tragedy as certainly provided noble examples, as Aristotle is certainly the best authority, since he it was who first explicitly, and with invincible argument, showed that unity in this sense is the essential thing in tragedy : and that not only as drama, but as the type of all literary composition. But as for the unities of time and place (which may, of course, in practice be invaluable for producing a certain kind of dramatic effect, as we may see in Racine's tragedy or Ben Jonson's comedy), the dogma which ascribes any *necessity* to these is purely arbitrary ; a good instance of those " rules " of criticism which, not being governed by genuinely philosophical theory, are merely misleading. In this case, the rules were governed by nothing but pedantry ; and, as it happened, by mistaken pedantry. The supposed example of Greek tragedy turns out to be by no means absolute ; and Aristotle, properly understood, provides no authority whatever. As regards time, no prescription of the *necessity* of the so-called unity can be made out from his carefully qualified remark on the practice of Greek drama ; and as regards place, a mere allusion in quite a different context is the only passage that can be alleged—and must be most fantastically wrested from its plain meaning to give any support to the dogma. No more absurd injustice was ever done to a critic than the suggestion that Aristotle would have condemned Shakespeare's dramatic treatment of time and place. If Shakespeare's plays satisfy unity of action, Aristotle would have required no more ; for the theory of poetry requires no more.

Aristotle now proceeds by focusing everything he has said hitherto into a formal definition of tragedy ; which definition his argument then elaborates, clause by clause, into a full exposition of the nature and function of tragedy. This definition, it is important to observe, is not offered as an *a priori* assertion of what tragedy ought to be ; it is a summary statement of what Aristotle has noted that tragedy actually is. After giving the definition, we shall merely give the gist of his exposition of it, without attempting to follow exactly the course of his argument, which is here rather tortuous and complicated. This portion of the treatise is the central doctrine of Aristotle's whole theory, and it is important for our purposes that it should be put as plainly as possible, though his elaborate argument will doubtless thereby lose some weight.

The definition of tragedy, then, is this : Tragedy is the imitation of an action that is serious, complete in itself, and possessing a certain magnitude ; in language that gives delight appropriate to each portion of the work ; in the form of drama, not of narrative ; through pity and fear accomplishing its *Katharsis* of such emotions.

This is a close paraphrase rather than an exact translation : but Aristotle's somewhat harsh concision of language defies exact translation as effectively as the finest lyricism of Sappho or Catullus. It will be seen that the definition falls into two divisions. In the first, consisting of the first three clauses, the *nature* of tragedy is given ; and this corresponds to the threefold classification with which the *Poetics* begins. The nature of tragedy is defined by that which is imitated—the object ; by that in which the imitation occurs—the medium ; and by the manner—how the imitation occurs. The second division consists of the final clause of the definition, which gives the *function* of tragedy. The crucial word here is the Greek word

Katharsis. Aristotle, as we have seen, held that, in order truly to understand tragedy, it was as necessary to understand its function as to understand its nature. That function, he now says, is a *Katharsis* ; but what *Katharsis* is, he entirely omits to explain. The meaning of the word is ambiguous ; it may be either " purgation " or " purification." Which sense does he intend ? And exactly what force does he intend the word to have in whichever sense is the right one ? For in either case the word is a metaphor. For the present it will be best to leave the word untranslated.

Our first business, then, is to collect Aristotle's idea of the nature of tragedy. We must next try to make out what he meant by *Katharsis* as the term for its function. If we cannot find that he meant anything really satisfactory, we must then try to draw from his idea of the nature of tragedy some idea of its function corresponding with the sort of function Aristotle intended the word *Katharsis* to indicate. We may perhaps find something for which, with a change of the metaphor, the term *Katharsis* may still be used. If so, and if it is a function which genuinely arises out of Aristotle's idea of the nature of tragedy, the whole resulting view of tragedy may properly be called the Aristotelian theory of tragedy : and it must justify itself not merely by offering itself as a theory of Greek tragedy, not merely as a theory of tragedy in general, but as a typical theory of literature.

We therefore now take up, and expand the implications of, Aristotle's definition of tragedy as it is given above. Tragedy is an imitation of an action. By an *action* here is meant an event, or process of events —something happening. But by calling it an *action*, what is also meant is, that this happens by means of, and in the being of, *agents*—agents which have a disposition to act. These agents are, of course, human beings : and their disposition to act is their *character*. The action, then, of which tragedy is an imitation, is a process of events embodied in the lives and wills of human beings. But tragedy is an imitation of an action that is complete in itself, and of a certain magnitude. " Complete in itself," simply means, that the action in itself forms a whole ; and " of a certain magnitude " simply means, that it can be *accepted* as a whole—it is neither too small to be appreciable, nor too large to be taken

in, as a whole. But to be a whole, it must
have a beginning, a middle, and an end.
There must be a definite point at which
the process of events as such begins, a
definite point at which the process as such
comes to an end. Before the first point, the
process did not exist : it now comes into
existence. After the last point, it finishes :
the process no longer exists. And in between these two points, the process co-
herently develops out of its beginning into
its end.

Such is the *object* of tragic imitation. And
it is at once evident that tragic imitation
is not the imitation of nature ; for such is
not the process of natural events. In
nature, nothing at any assignable point
begins, and nothing at any assignable
point comes to an end : all is perfect continuity. What tragedy imitates is not life,
but a conception of life : a very different
matter. Some possibility of life is seized
on by the poet's mind, and imagined as
a single movement of events. Some sense
of life has become, by intense imaginative
attention to it, clarified and defined into an
idea of life—an idea shaping itself forth in
the action of life ; and the action has the
unity of the idea it manifests. The idea, in

fact, is what we have previously called the inspiration : " action " is Aristotle's technical term for imaginative inspiration in the case of drama. And however complex the idea may be, it must be a unity ; otherwise it could not be attended to as an idea. The imaginative form it takes—the action, the movement of events—must be equally a unity : and in that essential respect must be unlike any movement of events in actual life.

Tragedy is the imitation of this. " Imitation," as we have seen, means, in Aristotle's theory, the technique by which this inspiration is communicably expressed, and the technique is defined by its medium, which is language, and its manner, which is drama : that is to say, tragedy is enacted before us by speaking persons, the persons whose behaviour *is* the tragedy. But when we consider what this involves, we see that the language, the tragic dialogue, is only, as it were, the final imitation : actually, there must be a whole series of imitations before the technique can arrive at the stage of language. This series of imitations can be set out in a scheme of the order of their importance, or of their proximity to the originating *action* : but

Aristotle's scheme is only for convenience of discussion ; the business could hardly occur in this schematic fashion. First, then, the action—that sense of life which the poet thinks of as some characteristic kind of movement of events—the imagined action expresses itself in the *plot*, or the arrangement of the incidents. The plot is then expressed in *characters* ; the *characters* in their *thoughts and feelings* ; and these finally in the dialogue or *language*. The truth of this scheme is very simply tested : all we have to do is to note what happens in us when we witness a tragedy. This, of course, exactly reverses the order of Aristotle's scheme : an order, once more, which is not meant to represent the process of composition, but merely the theory of the art. But in taking in the art, and critically appreciating it, we first receive the language ; the language gives us the thoughts and feelings of the persons speaking, by which we understand their behaviour ; from this we come to perceive their characters, and the characters embody the plot. Doubtless it is impossible to exaggerate the importance of the language ; since it is the language which must finally convey the whole series of the

dramatist's technique. That is why dramatic language cannot be the speech of actual
life, which never has any such burden laid
on it : the dialogue of drama must always
be unusually (it would be correct to say,
unnaturally) expressive. But however we
look at drama, whether we approach it
theoretically, from its motive, or critically,
from its effect, our conclusion must be the
same : namely, that the most important
thing in its technique is the plot.

Aristotle asserts this with the greatest
possible emphasis. " The plot," he says,
" is the first principle, and, as it were, the
soul of a tragedy : character comes second." The assertion is strikingly at vari-
ance with the assumption of many dramatic critics, who regard a dramatist first and
foremost as a creator of character. But,
says Aristotle, character by itself, however
skilfully delineated, will never give tragedy : it is only character in action that
can be tragic (or, more generally, dramatic). Characterization is, in fact, as
much a part of the dramatist's expressive
technique as the prosody or imagery of
his language ; and what he is expressing is
the idea of life which inspires him. The
assumption that his chief business is to

draw character is merely a relic of the
naïve and unexamined belief that drama
imitates life. It imitates a conception of
life ; and characterization is but a phase of
this imitation. This conception is what
Aristotle calls the action ; and the essence
of the action is its unity. It is the plot that
expresses the action ; all the rest of the
dramatist's technique—character, thought,
and language—embodies the plot. It is by
means of the plot that, theoretically considered, the whole mass of the drama is
held in the unity of the dramatist's inspiration ; and it is by means of the plot
that, critically considered, the whole mass
of the play falls into a unity of effect.

But the definition of tragedy requires a
further limitation. The action it imitates or
expresses must not only be a unity ; it must
also be serious. " Serious " is hardly an
adequate rendering of Aristotle's pregnant
epithet ; but what he means is made perfectly clear by his statement that tragedy
must arouse the emotions of pity and fear :
whereby we pass from his definition of its
nature to that of its function. We must
remind ourselves here of Aristotle's implied opposition to Plato. For it was
against the function of tragedy, and

precisely against its function as rousing pity and fear, that Plato brought his gravest charge. We have already seen how the Aristotelian doctrine of imitation gives a complete answer to Plato's accusation, that poetry is an unnecessary, superfluous, and unworthy form of activity. The whole force of the accusation there is derived from a misunderstanding of the imitativeness of poetry, and vanishes as soon as the true nature of poetic imitation is shown. So far, Aristotle's account of tragedy, by bringing out the full import of his doctrine of imitation, has made his case against Plato in this respect unanswerable. For no one can deny that to define tragedy as the imitation of an action in Aristotle's sense, with all that Aristotle finds implied in that definition, is simply to describe, with unmistakable accuracy, the nature of tragedy as it actually exists. But Plato also charged poetry, and notably tragedy, with having a radically vicious effect, due to its power of exciting emotion ; and this much more considerable charge Aristotle opposes by his doctrine of *Katharsis*. All the rest of his treatise is governed by the doctrine : whatever else he has to say about tragedy involves its *function*—which

indeed could not but be of the first importance to a philosopher of Aristotle's
outlook and predilection. Unfortunately,
the idea of *Katharsis* was so familiar to
him, and doubtless to his pupils, that he
never stops to explain it. Even more than
was the case with " imitation," we must
make out what the word means by the
way he uses it.

But first we must understand what
Plato's charge against tragedy was.
Roughly, it is this. How does a tragic hero
arouse our emotions ? By bewailing his
misfortunes : the more he can make us feel
his grief, the more we admire him. Now
in real life, the man we admire, and
rightly, is the man who, without com-
plaining, endures misfortune and con-
trols its effect on him. Who would not be
ashamed to indulge his lamentation, and
to press his affliction on his neighbours ?
Can it be right to admire an actor for
doing the very things we despise in real
life ? Moreover, by giving way to sympathy with him, we enjoy these lamentable
emotions ; sorrow becomes facile ; pity, by
weakening our control over grievous feelings, encourages us to indulge them also in
the case of our own misfortunes. The whole

effect of tragedy tends to debility of spirit :
reason relaxes its hold on conduct, emotion takes charge.

Aristotle does not attempt to challenge
(as he did in the case of the imitativeness
of tragedy) the facts on which Plato
grounds his accusation here. He agrees
that it is characteristic of tragedy to arouse
emotions which, in themselves, are danger-
ous, and perhaps unwholesome. Indeed,
he is clearly wrong in agreeing too closely
with Plato in this respect ; for though pity
and fear are certainly important among
the tragic emotions, they are not the only
tragic emotions : love and admiration are
equally important in the effect of tragedy.
But of the emotions he names, everyone
would admit that fear is not an emotion to
be encouraged for its own sake ; and
probably Aristotle had the same opinion
of pity : at any rate, excess of pity, like
excess of anything else, he would regard
with strong disfavour. But, says Aristotle,
tragedy not only rouses these emotions ;
it also, by the way it rouses them, effects
a *Katharsis* of them. This is his answer to
Plato.

Katharsis is in any case a metaphor. It
may allude to rites of religion, in which

case it means "purification" ; or it may
allude to theories of medicine, in which
case it means "purgation." It is not easy
to see exactly what is meant by "purify-
ing" pity and fear ; though something
vaguely analogous with this sense may
commend itself more plausibly as the sort
of function Aristotle had in his mind, than
that on which he actually insisted. For it
seems certain that "purification" was not
what he himself meant by *Katharsis*. Whenever he alludes to the tragic *Katharsis*, this
is evidently identical with the mere fact of
rousing pity and fear. There is never any
hint of a "purification" of these emotions. But if he meant "purgation," it
would be quite enough to refer to *Katharsis*
as the mere rousing of these emotions. In
Greek medicine, an organism could be
purged of any undesirable product by the
administration, in judicious doses, of something similar : as in modern homeopathy,
"like cures like." Excess of any kind was
unwholesome ; health could be secured by
purgation of anything which tended to be
present in excess. This seems to be what
Aristotle meant by *Katharsis*. Tragedy
effected the purgation of pity and fear, by
its administration of these very emotions :

107

it was desirable that these emotions should be discharged, either because they were unwholesome in themselves, or because they tended to excess. Confirmation of this is given by what Aristotle says elsewhere of the effect of music. Certain highly exciting kinds of music have, he asserts, the effect of calming those who are already in a state of high excitement : by the administration of like emotion, their excessive emotion is purged away, and the process, he notes, is accompanied by feelings of pleasure. That this was Aristotle's own interpretation of the doctrine of *Katharsis* was well understood by Milton, who seems to have been the first English writer to explain it precisely. In the preface to *Samson Agonistes*, Milton calls tragedy the "most profitable of all other poems" ; and supports this opinion by invoking the authority of Aristotle in these terms : "therefore said by Aristotle to be of power by raising pity and fear, or terror, to purge the mind of those and such like passions, that is to temper and reduce them to just measure with a kind of delight, stirred up by reading or seeing those passions well imitated. Nor is Nature wanting in her own effects to make good his assertion : for so in Physic things of melancholic hue and quality are used against melancholy, sour against sour, salt to remove salt humours." Here we touch the medieval version of Greek medical theory. But there can be no doubt that Milton was entirely right : Aristotle regarded the function of tragedy as something medical : the pity and fear of tragedy were the doses by which the tragic poet homeopathically purged his audience into emotional health.

The medical analogy, of course, means nothing to us, except as a curiosity. But it is not for that reason that the theory fails ; there might be something in it, which would stand, without any analogy to support it. The theory, however, is unsound in itself. What Aristotle says of music may be true ; but in that case, the persons who were cured by ecstatic music were already possessed by ecstasy. But an audience does not go into a theatre in a state of pity and fear. Everyone is liable to these emotions ; but they are not present unless they are provoked. Tragedy, in order to be curative, must first produce the disease it is to cure. Yet we must surely feel that Aristotle's explanation of the function of tragedy was an attempt in the right direction. Tragedy certainly does produce an enjoyable and wholesome effect, by rousing in us emotions which in real life would be unpleasantly and perhaps dangerously disturbing (though these are not the only emotions it rouses). And the earlier part of Aristotle's theory—that which expounds the nature of tragedy—will give us a sufficient explanation of this remarkable effect : which, for the sake of convenience, we may still call *Katharsis*, though not now in the medical sense, and not exactly in the religious sense of " purification." But in so far as the emotions roused by the spectacle of the evil in life—not merely moral evil, but the evil of destruction and waste and misfortune—are by tragedy deprived of evil effect, and even made beneficial, something like " purification " may be alleged.

We return to that quality which Aristotle showed to be essential in the nature of tragedy—its *unity*. It is from this quality that he deduces his famous assertion, that " poetry is a more philosophical and a nobler thing than history." That is to say, poetry is more in accordance with the spirit of philosophy, the instinctive desire to *understand* : which means, the desire to

know the laws of things, and to generalize
these laws as widely as possible—to proceed from knowing how one thing is connected with another, to knowing how all
things are connected together. Now history relates what has actually happened :
things happened just so, but *why* they happened just so we can never be sure, for we
can never account for all the antecedents
of an actual event, nor reckon up all its
consequences. We can surmise the law of
the event, but we can never know it. But
poetry relates what may happen according to the law of probability or necessity.
We know what happens and we know
how it happens. In contrast with history,
in which nothing begins and nothing ends,
and in which the mere sequence of events
must satisfy as best it may our desire to
know the secret connexion of events, in
poetry we see an event complete in itself,
definitely beginning and definitely ending
and proceeding with perfect coherence
from antecedents we understand to consequences we accept as inevitable. While we
live in the event, we live in the world we
most profoundly desire ; our consciousness of things takes the form of a world in
which all things are connected together.

Now tragedy exhibits the misfortune of life. But by reason of the unity of tragic drama, even the misfortune of life becomes an instance of the world we most profoundly desire. This accounts for the peculiar pleasure we take in tragedy. Things which in real life would be merely distressing become in tragedy nobly exhilarating. They do not cease to be distressing ; but something is added to this ; whereby their evil becomes our good. Even in evil, we gain the world we need. And in this sense, tragedy may be said to effect a *Katharsis* of the emotions it rouses. It is not the *Katharsis* Aristotle meant ; but it is entirely in accordance with what Aristotle says. It is also in accordance with the facts.

All the rest of the *Poetics* is governed by Aristotle's idea of *Katharsis* as the function of tragedy. Wherever the idea is valid, our interpretation of it will be found workable : which is not surprising, since it is an interpretation Aristotle himself might well have given. But his insistence on pity and fear leads him sometimes to emphasize sensationalism in tragedy, and sometimes serves to excuse the prejudices of his philosophical system. A celebrated example

of the latter is his account of the hero
or heroine proper to tragedy. A tragic
character is one that passes from pros-
perity to adversity. This must not be, says
Aristotle, because he is a villain : that
would arouse neither pity nor fear. But it
must not be the unmerited misfortune of
a perfectly virtuous character : that would
be merely shocking. The tragic character
must be something in between these two
extremes : a person who is good, but not
eminently good, and who brings on himself misfortune by his own error. This is
simply Aristotle's doctrine of the " golden
mean " intruding where it has no business. " The practice of the stage," he says,
" bears us out." It did no such thing in
his day, and has never done any such
thing since. The character Aristotle describes may certainly be a tragic character;
but equally tragic may be an utter villain,
like Macbeth, who deserves all his misfortune, or a perfectly innocent person,
like Desdemona, who deserves none of it.

Yet so great is Aristotle's prestige, that
critics in all succeeding ages have attempted to reduce the practice of the
dramatists to his theory of tragic character.
Thus, it is pointed out that in the tragedy

Hc   113

of *Prometheus Bound*, Æschylus has drawn
a noble hero who nevertheless has grave
faults. This is quite true ; but the whole
point of the tragedy—the thing that makes
it perhaps the greatest of all tragedies—is
that Prometheus does not suffer for his
faults, but for his virtues : it is because of
the good he has done that the Power which
rules the world condemns him. Of course,
any act that goes wrong may be called an
error ; but this is not what Aristotle means.
For him, the tragic error (which he at
one point says must be a *great* error) is
quite plainly a moral lapse, not a mere
failure to calculate all possible consequences. The truth is, that he ignored, in
the interests of his theory, the unmistakably tragic effect of innocence suffering
undeservedly, of Right punished by Wrong
—and punished for *being* Right. If his
theory of tragic function had taken into
account its rousing of love and admiration
as well as of pity and fear, he would
scarcely have failed to perceive the tragic
possibilities in the suffering of innocence.
Perhaps also he would have done justice
to the other case which he denies to be
tragedy—the opposite case of the downfall
of the heroic villain. For, as *Macbeth* shows

us, it is possible to admire a villain; possible even to feel for him a sympathy which is not, in the end, very far from love. But much more interesting than attempts to apply Aristotle's rule to cases which obviously contradict it, is the modification of it which Hegel suggested as the true doctrine of the tragic person : though here again æsthetic theory doubtless recommended itself to its author for its convenient accordance with his general philosophy. Certainly, says Hegel, the nature of tragedy allows a character to suffer for being in the right ; and yet the suffering may be just. For the right may not be an absolute right. It may be valid in ordinary circumstances ; but there may also be circumstances in which it is irreconcilably opposed by another equally valid right. Both are right ; but each is right only from its own point of view. The stock instance is Sophocles's tragedy of *Antigone*. Antigone's brother has committed the worst possible crime against his country, and has been killed in the act. Kreon, the ruler of Thebes, has refused him the rites of burial ; thus answering one atrocious wrong by another equally atrocious. Antigone contrives to pay the rites demanded by religion to her brother's corpse ; and is punished, as she knew she would be, by death. She appeals to the " unwritten laws " which man's conscience must obey against all earthly laws ; but Kreon appeals to the laws which the State has a right to make in vindication of its existence. Now, says Hegel, Antigone is in the right ; but only from her point of view ; she represents the rights of individual conscience. But Kreon is equally right from his point of view ; he represents the rights of the State. The conflict is irreconcilable. Both must suffer ; that is the tragedy.

This, like Aristotle's theory, is one of the possible cases of tragedy : but it no more provides a universal rule than Aristotle does. The *Antigone* itself does not bear it out ; though Hegel's theory certainly reminds us that, in order to understand Sophocles's tragedy, we must sympathize with Kreon as well as with Antigone. But the tragedy is, nevertheless, that Antigone is right and Kreon is wrong : and that the wrong has power to condemn the right. However plausible, and indeed profound, Hegel's theory may be, perhaps there is no tragedy that exactly accords with it.

But the whole age-long discussion is a good instance of how criticism may be misled by a theory which, however philosophical elsewhere, is not truly philosophical in *art* : a theory, that is to say, which, professing to interpret the facts, only does so by presenting facts which it can interpret.

With the rest of Aristotle's treatise we need not further concern ourselves ; though it is all eminently worth the carefullest study. But we now have the main features of his theory of tragedy : which, once more, is to be understood as a type of the theory of literary art in general. He illustrates it by working it out in detail in many interesting and important directions ; and he shows how it can be transposed from the dramatic to the narrative manner—from tragedy to epic. It is enough for our purpose to have explained the general nature of his poetic theory. For, whatever may be said against it here and there, Aristotle's theory of tragedy is the foundation on which all subsequent discussion of literary æsthetic has most securely based itself.

IV. AFTER ARISTOTLE

IV. AFTER ARISTOTLE

No ATTEMPT will be made in this
section to sketch, however cursorily, anything like a connected history of literary
criticism since Aristotle. Even if we confined ourselves to English literature, it
would not be possible here to describe the
criticism of all those authors who have
achieved marked eminence in this kind of
writing. Nor, indeed, would it serve our
purpose. The criticism of literature is often
as entirely individual as the creation of
literature, and as much the work of in-
definable genius. Its success may be due
to talents which do not require, and certainly do not seek—which perhaps would
indignantly repel—the support of philosophical principles. Insight, sympathy,
imaginative response, common sense, or
mere power to express discriminating
gusto—of these abilities, and other such,
may excellent criticism be made, without
anything being formulated. We may call
this intuitive criticism. Our concern, however, will be with the criticism which is

notable not merely for its quality, but for its addition to, or confirmation of, the intelligible *methods* of criticism. We shall attempt no more than a summary account of several tendencies in the history of criticism, briefly noticing some important contributions to its rational tradition. This means that we shall be concerned with critics who have been at least aware that there is such a thing as literary theory, even though they may not have been inclined to formulate it ; similarly, we shall only mention theorists whose doctrines have proved, in one way or another, of value to criticism.

Horace is typical of the critic who has a *method*, which he is prepared to set out in a more or less systematic body of rules, independent of actual cases of the critical estimation of literature. Such a method evidently supposes a theory underlying it ; but Horace is also typical of the critic who does not trouble to expound his theory ; he is quite content if the rules themselves provide reasonable guidance. The theory underlying the *Ars Poetica*[1] is substantially

[1] A good prose translation by Fairclough in the Loeb Library (Heinemann), and a lively metrical version by Conington (Bell).

Aristotle's ; but Horace's interest in it is not in the least philosophical, but purely practical ; he accepts it for what he, as a critic, can make of it. Thus the poem is in no sense an argument ; it is a collection of precepts and pieces of advice, somewhat abruptly put together, and always with a connexion that is more poetical than logical. For it must be remembered that the *Ars Poetica* is not primarily a work of criticism ; first and foremost it is a poem—a poem on the subject of criticism. And the chief value of its subject is in the poetry it urges Horace to write. There is more to be learnt from its workmanship than from its precepts. Perhaps no poem of comparable length has provided so many phrases that have become the common property of international culture. Here is the " purple patch " ; here " Homer nods " ; here the critic exclaims " *incredulus odi* " ; and here the old man is " *laudator temporis acti.*" The context of that last phrase is a good instance of the way Horace treats his subject. A character, he says, must accord with what we know of life ; it must, for instance, be suited to the supposed age of the person represented. And at once he

123

proceeds to a brilliant summary of the changes in human nature with the process of time ; finally arriving at his pregnant, pathetic, and cruel picture of old age. He has forgotten all about literary criticism. It is the poet who knows the world, and who can distil his knowledge into a quintessence of language, that is writing now.

But these memorable phrases are not always, in relation to his discussion of criticism, merely ornamental. Their real point is sometimes lost when they are removed, not so much from their logical, as from their poetical context. When an author seizes on an opportunity for fine writing, we talk of a " purple patch." But that is not quite what Horace meant. He disapproved of the " purple patch " that was " *sewn on* " : that was not, therefore, an integral part of the texture of the whole. And this is typical of his critical method. Throughout the *Ars Poetica*, the governing consideration is the essential doctrine of Aristotle's *Poetics*, the doctrine of Unity. And it is the genuine Unity which Horace maintains : Unity of action, as it came to be called ; Unity of substance, of mood, of effect, as Horace maintains it. This is the chief debt which the tradition of criticism owes to the *Ars Poetica* : it was Horace who made the spirit of Aristotle's theory the ideal of European criticism. Horace was read when Aristotle was not ; even when Aristotle's influence in Europe was at its height, Horace was infinitely more readable than Aristotle ; his witty epigrams, deliciously phrased, disseminated the doctrine as Aristotle's compact and elliptical reasoning never could have done. It was Horace, in fact, who made men feel that the demand for Unity in a work of art is identical with *good taste* ; and this was not recommending a certain fashion in taste ; it was simply making men conscious of what good taste really is. A sound philosophy of art is nothing but a rational account of good taste. Horace, by transforming Aristotle's doctrine into critical rules, philosophically enlightened good taste without troubling his readers to philosophize about it. His immense influence in the history of criticism is, indeed, precisely due to the fact that he made æsthetic theory *appeal* to good taste.

Except in one important particular, he has nothing of his own to add to the

Poetics. He is, in fact, a thoroughly conservative critic : it may be counted against him, that he is chiefly responsible for the wholly false notion, that classicism means conservatism. But his conservatism is easily explicable. The example of the Greek poets, he says, must be studied night and day. Poetry must still be composed as they composed it. For instance, the characters they gave to the great figures of myth and legend must be exactly maintained. Horace thinks that this respect for the ancients leaves quite sufficient room for originality ; and he apparently forgets the extraordinary liberties the Greek dramatists allowed themselves to take with the psychology of their heroes. But it is not easy for us to realize how completely Roman culture in Horace's day was dominated by Greek models and Greek standards. The very idea of literature might almost be said to be a Greek idea transported to Rome ; certainly that could be said of literature as an activity cultivated for its own sake—of literature, so to speak, conscious of itself as an art. There was, for Horace, only one safe way in literature : and that was the Greek way. This is simply the historical situation of Roman culture translated into opinion. When we find, in a totally different situation, Pope recommending a similar respect for the ancients, the grounds for this respect have completely changed. Pope has to give plausible reasons for it. Horace is aware of no such necessity. For him, if literature is to exist at all, it must be on the Greek model : the reason why Greek standards must be accepted in literature is identical with the reason why there is such a thing as literature. And that, being a philosophical question, is no concern of his. He simply assumes (quite rightly) that the doctrine he expounds contains the answer.

But Horace had another and more salutary excuse for his conservatism. The *Ars Poetica* is, in form, a body of precepts addressed to those who wish to compose poetry. He detested the notion that poetry is something eccentric ; though Aristotle himself is partially responsible for the belief that poetry and madness are allied. Horace abhorred the poets whose " inspiration " took the form of crazy behaviour either in their art or in their conduct. The rage for extreme individualism provoked in him his sturdiest conservatism ; and his determined assertion that a poet must be a rational being, and poetry a rational art, is not the least of his services to sound criticism. Thus, under the appearance of advising poets how to criticize their own compositions, his real intention is to declare the true nature of literary merit ; and his rules and precepts for self-criticism become applicable to the criticism of literature in general.

But in one matter, Horace is remarkably liberal ; and that he is so in this particular matter is an excellent instance of his sanity as a critic. This is the matter of diction. Aristotle's treatment of this is very disappointing. But Horace's is exactly right ; and unfortunately it is just here that his wisdom has, in the history of criticism, been least influential : though nowadays it is just here that it might seem most valuable. Poetic diction, he says, can never be an altogether established and stationary affair. The function of language in poetry is to express ; but man's experience, which poetry exists to express, is continually changing, since it is continually adding to itself. With the growth of experience, the language of poetry must keep pace, if it is

to be truly expressive. Language is like
a tree ; and its words are like the leaves.
As the years go on, the old leaves fall, and
new leaves take their place : but the tree
remains the same. Horace's simile nicely
puts the case of language and its words in
the art of literature. But we must remember that in the trees which Horace
had in mind, all the old leaves do not fall
off at once ; thus at any moment, the
leafage consists of both old and new. So it
must be with poetic language. New words
must be continually coming in, and old
words dropping out. The poet must not
expect to rely wholly on the proved poetic
vocabulary of his predecessors, and he
must not be afraid of being the first to
make poetic use of new words. But of
course, as Horace admirably points out,
there is always the possibility, by skilfully
joining words together in phrases, of
making quite new poetic use of the most
familiar words. Much fallacious writing
and thinking about poetic diction would
have been saved, if this exquisite passage,
which is as true to the nature of language
as it is to the nature of poetry, had had
on subsequent criticism anything like the
influence of his doctrine that Five Acts

Ic   129

in Drama are prescribed by an absolute rule.

On the whole, if we judge by effect, the most important name in the history of criticism next to Aristotle is Horace. Criticism which can give a rational account of itself was first made possible by Aristotle's philosophy ; but it was the *Ars Poetica* which broadcast the seed of the *Poetics* over every literature in Europe. In the *Poetics*, the efficacy of Aristotle's doctrine depends on his reader's ability to follow philosophical reasoning ; in the *Ars Poetica*, the magic of poetry has released it from this severe condition : henceforth the doctrine, or the essential spirit of it, is something which can *be enjoyed*. And the whole world has enjoyed it. What the history of criticism owes to Horace is quite inestimable. Of no other figure, in the rest of our summary, will it be necessary to speak so fully.

In the scale which our survey requires, after Horace the next great figure in the critical succession is *Dante*.[1] For Dante, Aristotle was " the master of those who know " ; but this was not the Aristotle who

[1] The works mentioned are translated in the Temple Classics edition (Dent).

wrote the *Poetics*. Dante knew no such Aristotle. He knew Horace ; but his philosophical mind required more than the *Ars Poetica* could give him. Possessed by the merciless rationalism of the middle ages, no rules could be valid for him without the theory on which they were grounded. But his theory was mainly theological, and is to-day not much more than an intellectual curiosity. Yet he can startle us with such complete anticipations, precisely argued, of modern theory, as his division of the power of language into " *signum rationale* " and " *signum sensuale* " ; which is exactly our quite recent distinction of " semantic " and " phonetic." And his division is reasoned from profound insight into the nature of language. No doubt his chief contribution to criticism, though its importance is only historical, is his defence of a national vernacular in literature against the specious claims of the universal language of learning, Latin. His account, in the unfinished *De Vulgari Eloquentia*, of the structure of vernacular lyrical forms, is of great value to literary history. But his attempt to found a noble vernacular diction on an æsthetic classification of words is nothing ; it was the poet

131

in him, not the theorist, who made Italian a match for the language of Homer or Virgil. Much more interesting, and vastly more important, is his assertion, elaborated in the unfinished *Convivio*, and succinctly given in the letter to Can Grande della Scala, of the symbolic meaning of poetry. This is an invaluable supplement to Aristotle's theory. For Dante, the " action " or story, which inspires a poem, means more to the poet than its merely human events ; it has seized on his mind because it seems to symbolize for him some conviction or intuition of the inmost meaning of life. According to Aristotle, the art of a poem is the symbol (or " imitation ") of its inspiration—its " action " ; and now, according to Dante, the action is itself symbolic. So that the whole poem not only embodies the action in artistic shape and substance, but by so doing suggests the symbolic (or, as Dante calls it, in a broad use of the word, the " allegorical ") significance of the action. This may not be a universal rule ; but its enlargement of Aristotle's system of " imitations " is clearly required in order to account for the full effect of such poems as the *Æneid* and *Paradise Lost* and *Gerusalemme*

Liberata, as well as of Dante's own *Divine Comedy.* The symbolic nature of human events as the inspiration of poetry is even more evident in lyrical poetry. The emotional moment which a lyric celebrates may to the poet mean much more than itself; and if it is completely caught in language, it will suggest this to the reader also. Dante himself is the great exemplar here : his love for Beatrice meant immeasurably more to him than merely human passion ; it was a symbol of matters transcending mortality. What these matters were, Dante endeavoured to expound, largely in terms of the scholastic philosophy. But they cannot be expounded : only the sense of them can be conveyed when the art of poetry is capable of conveying the very life of the moment that inspired it. Thus, for the higher criticism of certain noble kinds of literature, Dante's doctrine of the " allegorical " nature of poetry is indispensable. There are many novels in which the action is as symbolical as the *Æneid* itself of matters not otherwise expressible.

Much of the criticism of the Renaissance was deeply concerned with the *Poetics.* The main contribution of the Renaissance to

133

the history of criticism was, in fact, the recovery of Aristotle's æsthetic philosophy for the modern world : though, as we have seen, the spirit of that philosophy had long been effective in the generalized form of the rules and precepts of Horace's *Ars Poetica*. In the earlier stage of the Renaissance, indeed, Horace was still the sole authority ; a position from which only Aristotle could depose him. But that followed inevitably on the discovery and circulation of the *Poetics*. Renaissance criticism, however, added little of any value to Aristotle ; its chief business was to interpret him. But there was one direction in which Aristotle's theory could obviously be extended. Plato said poetry imitated Nature. No, said Aristotle ; it imitates a conception of Nature : and to that he confined his theory. But what is the relation between Nature as it is and Nature as the poet conceives it ? What does the poetical conception of Nature mean ? The answer is no doubt implied by Aristotle's theory ; but the Renaissance critics began to make it explicit. Thus Sir Philip Sidney, in his brilliant *Apologie*, insisting on the freedom of poetry, finds its proper business in its creation of a sort of counterpart to Nature, in which whatever may delight us exists in its perfection ; and Bacon more profoundly says that poetry " doth raise and erect the mind, by submitting the shows of things to the desires of the mind." Since the Renaissance, this is the direction in which what we may call Aristotelian æsthetic theory has tended to develop. With Kant, the Baconian " desires of the mind " became the desire for a representation of the purpose in things ; but poetry, he says, represents things as purposive without representing any distinct purpose. So, too, for Shelley, poetry has a moral effect, without recommending any specific morality. For morality is simply mental life at its highest and finest ; and the vitality of the mind is in its imagination, which poetry feeds. In poetry we live in the world out of which our sense of the purpose of things and the morality of action emerges : we live in the world which is immediately and on its own account, without reference to ulterior standards, significant. In what region of experience can this immediately satisfactory world occur ? Benedetto Croce gives the answer : it is in the region of pure intuition, of experience accepted for its own sake. The question of the *reality* of experience does not arise in this region : we are satisfied with the experience itself, simply as such. But Croce seems to limit his answer to sensuous and emotional intuition. Yet anything at all, even ratiocination, can be intuited and taken as pure experience. The conception of nature, then, which poetry represents (and poetry stands for the art of literature generally), is a conception of the world which we most profoundly desire, imagined simply as existing, and satisfying our desires simply by being so imagined. And what we most profoundly desire in the world is law and order. Any kind of pure literature is inspired by the conception of a world which merely has to exist in order to assure us that its existence is an affair of perfect interconnexion and coherence. This is true, however the inspiration is represented to imagination ; whether as short story, or novel, or drama, or epic, or lyric.

This is the more theoretical tendency in criticism. But also since the Renaissance another tendency, of at least equal importance, has been discernible—the criticism of literary style. The fountain-head of stylistic criticism is also a Greek treatise,

136

usually called *Longinus on the Sublime*[1] :
a work which has sometimes seemed to
rival in importance even the *Poetics.* But
it is a wholly critical work, making no
appeal to any philosophical theory of art.
Though the work of a Greek of the first
century, its importance in the history of
criticism is entirely modern, dating from
1554, when it was first printed ; it seems
to have been unknown to ancient or
medieval culture. The title is a double
misnomer : it is not by Longinus, and it is
not concerned, in our sense of the word,
with the Sublime. The anonymous author
was attempting to formulate the nature
and constitution of that style in literature
which " elevates " language above its ordinary uses. He was the first comparative
critic of literature ; for, besides Greek and
Roman, he could also draw from Hebrew
literature, quoting with admiration from
Moses ("no ordinary man "), as a sentence worthy of the Deity, " Let there be
light, and there was light." The great
merit of his treatment of literary style is,
that though he certainly regards it as
a quality on which criticism may fix its
attention, he never thinks of it as a mere

[1] Translated by Rhys Roberts (Cambridge University Press).

137

outer layer of decoration. Style, for " Longinus " (so, for convenience, we may continue to call the author), is the revelation of the very spirit of a work and of the personality of its author. The saying " Style is the man" takes its origin from " Longinus " : but he is too good a critic to leave it at that. Style is the man indeed : but the man doing a particular piece of work in a particular kind of mood. He attempts to classify the various causes in the nature of both work and poet, which can produce " elevated " style : the scheme is perhaps not quite satisfactory, but very suggestive. He thinks these " sources of elevation " (grandeur of conception, vehement passion, the ability rightly to employ certain definable modes of linguistic expression) should yield rules for good style : rules of such genuine authority that the breaking of them could be counted positive and unmistakable faults. Nothing should condone such faults ; for they are the true sins against good taste, offences against the finest harmony of poetry. But he admits that genius is not to be bound by rules ; though the admission does not compromise the validity of his rules. Faults are none the less faults for being committed by genius. But the headstrong energy of genius, which ignores rules and commits faults, is more likely to do valuable things in the whole result, than the cautious spirit which always remembers the rules, and will run no risk of offending good taste. Yet no poet, who wishes to make the most of his endowment, should be indifferent to rules—at any rate, to " art " in the sense of the conscious and rational management of his creative power. There are those who say poetic power is simply the gift of Nature. It undoubtedly is the gift of Nature, like good fortune. But just as, in order to use good fortune, good counsel is advisable, so the poet will be wise if he allows art to show him how best to use what Nature has given him.

In the criticism which we may call stylistic (taking style in the large sense which " Longinus " had given it), this attitude to poetry first becomes effective in English literature with Ben Jonson. Against the typical Elizabethan reliance on spontaneous, and often ungoverned, energy, Jonson upheld, by magnificent practice and vigorous precept, the ideal of poetry as creative power controlled by conscious, deliberate, and learned art : in which, however, abstract rules (the Unities of Time and Place, for instance, or the Five Acts in Drama) were only valid as they served a genuinely rational artistic purpose. When Elizabethan spontaneity failed, " strangled in its waste fertility," Jonson's was the ideal that survived into the succeeding ages ; and the " school of Ben " was powerfully confirmed in its general attitude by the criticism, vacillating in principle but always rational in method, of Dryden. But it was *Pope* who first in English literature attempted anything like a complete exposition of stylistic criticism. Like Horace's *Ars Poetica, An Essay on Criticism* is first and foremost a poem, and as poetry is primarily to be judged : and a most delightfully entertaining poem it is, as full as anything Pope ever did of his memorable wit and his exquisite skill with words. But it is a poem on the subject of criticism ; and of great importance in the history of that subject for its bringing together into one focus the influences of Aristotle, " Longinus," the school of Ben Jonson, Dryden, common sense, French ideals of literary taste, and the rationalism of Cartesian philosophy. Whence does criticism derive

its authority ? Pope combines into a single
mental attitude three authoritative ideas—
the idea of Nature, the idea of Antiquity,
the idea of Reason. All three must be
obeyed ; but this means no divided alle-
giane—rather the authority of each one
confirms the other two. " First follow
Nature " ; but to learn how to do this,
study the Ancients. For the Ancients were
at one with Nature ; Nature and the
Poetry of Antiquity are the same. But also
to study the Ancients is to study art that
always accords with reason : the lesson of
antiquity is that poetry must obey the
rules which reason prescribes. How is
this ? The answer is (and here comes in the
influence of that rationalism which the
immensely potent philosophy of Descartes
had made almost universal), Nature herself is reason. If Nature seems irrational,
it is our own understanding that is at fault.
The ancient poets portrayed a rational
world, because they knew what Nature
truly is. The rules of art which they obeyed
were not imposed on Nature ; the rules
were drawn from Nature—they were "dis-
covered, not devised," they were the laws
which Nature " first herself ordain'd " :
they were the very truth of Nature,

precisely because they were rational. If
there is any distinction to be drawn between art and nature, it is that art, being
rational, is more natural than Nature
herself—than the Nature, that is, of actual
experience.

This dogma (for of course it is nothing
more) that Nature is really identical with
reason, and that consequently Nature is
never so natural as in art (if art obeys the
ancient rules), is the keystone in Pope's
theory : a theory which may be described
as a lucid confusion of ideas. He did not
revere the Ancients, as Horace did, simply
because they were predecessors, who could
provide instructive instances of successful
poetic art ; he revered them because,
somehow, they possessed Nature's secret.
Aristotle had given a rational account of
their art ; and therefore their practice
must be rational. This is no doubt true,
though very far from the whole truth.
But Pope's theory does not amount to
more than this : that the nature which
poetry draws is the nature which we *desire*
to know. This gives us no more than Aristotle had given. But Pope is writing in
favour of a certain style of poetic composition—not only in language, but in

onception also. It is what we roughly call
he eighteenth century style of poetry ;
.nd since the theory of it could invoke
hree names of such authority as Nature,
\ntiquity, and Reason, it is no wonder
hat this style could outlast a whole cen-
ury—that it could begin in the seven-
eenth, prevail in the eighteenth, and
:ontinue well into the nineteenth century.

   But Pope, the editor of Shakespeare,
:ould not but admit that there might be
' glorious offenders " against the rules.
This admission is quite different from the
\pparently similar admission made by
' Longinus." With " Longinus," faults
were faults, whoever committed them.
But with Pope, the rules were such, that
\n offence against them might be an
:xcellence for which the rules had not
provided. For the rules can only give as
much as we can perceive of Nature's
reasonableness ; and genius may always
transcend our ordinary perception of this.
The admission that genius is *right* not to
be limited by the rules should, properly
speaking, deprive the rules of all their
supposed validity. They cannot, at least,
be more than provisionally valid.

   Eighteenth century poetic style is most

conspicuous in its diction. If poetry is always a rational art, must not the same kind of diction be always its most suitable medium ? Thus there came to prevail the belief that a certain kind of diction was, *per se*, poetical, and would be right for all poetical occasions : and the formation of a diction that seemed to satisfy these requirements was perhaps the most remarkable achievement of the eighteenth century. But in fact it was only really suited to a peculiar kind of rational inspiration. Revolt against it had been frequent, though sporadic, during the eighteenth century itself, and in 1800 its universal pretensions were exploded by Wordsworth's celebrated Preface to *Lyrical Ballads*. Wordsworth denied that there can be any such thing as diction poetical *per se* ; the proper language for poetry is the " language really used by men," which becomes poetical by the way it is used. Like most reforms, this goes too far in the opposite direction ; and Wordsworth himself in his practice never hesitated, when it suited his purpose, to use language which belongs to literature rather than to life. But his protest remains invaluable ; after Wordsworth, the tradition of criticism

approves the use of any language in literature which will serve the writer's turn.
Properly speaking, there is only one fault
to be found with style : failure to be expressive in the sense of being truly, finely,
and vividly communicative. Wordsworth
cleared the way for the Romantics and all
subsequent movements towards liberty of
style. But the lesson of the eighteenth century has not therefore been lost : the
tradition of criticism still bears the impress
of its tremendous emphasis on the ideal of
" Longinus " and Ben Jonson. Whether
Nature is rational or not, poetry must be ;
not necessarily logically or scientifically,
but artistically, rational. It must be an
activity which is wholly and completely
designed.

Mention of the Romantics brings us to
the third main tendency in the tradition
of criticism ; though, like Romanticism
itself, it begins long before anything like
a Romantic Movement is discernible. This
too may be due to the influence of Descartes : at any rate, it belongs to something
much wider than literature and its criticism. It forms part of the increasing importance in modern consciousness of the
distinction between the subjective and the

objective elements of experience, between the person that experiences and the world that is experienced, between " inner " and " outer " life. This tendency may be most suitably approached, perhaps, through its addition of a new category to critical valuation. This is the category of the Sublime, in the sense in which Coleridge uses the word, when he claims Sublimity to be the peculiar distinction of Hebrew literature as against Greek or Roman. The suggestion is that Sublimity is somehow superior to mere beauty.

The category of the Sublime first decisively enters the critical tradition with Burke's *A philosophical inquiry into the origin of our ideas of the Sublime and Beautiful* (1756). Neither the theoretical nor Aristotelian tendency in criticism, nor the stylistic tendency which derives from " Longinus," would give any justification to the assertion, that the *purpose* of poetry is to be beautiful ; but in both it would be right to say, that when poetry succeeds in its purpose, it is *judged* to be beautiful. But may there not be, asks Burke, something better than beauty in poetry ? Is not passion more important than beauty? This implies a somewhat limited understanding of the word beauty, which becomes more evident as the tendency goes on. For Burke, beauty is to be defined in such terms as " delicacy," " smoothness," " grace," even " smallness." His argument goes thus. The free exercise of any emotion is in itself pleasant ; and the greater the emotion, the greater the pleasure. Even emotions associated with painful or terrible things are, as emotions, pleasant, provided they are disinterested. In poetry, that is precisely what they are : the painful and terrible things in poetry do not happen to us : we contemplate them, and are only affected by the emotions which accompany them. These emotions can then be freely enjoyed ; and those are found to be most moving which accompany ideas or suggestions of death, destruction, annihilation, immensity, the unbounded, the infinite. That which astonishes and overwhelms us with its emotional effect is what we call the Sublime : and this effect is usually produced by something which is incapable of apprehension. The effect is, indeed, that of terror ; " terror is in all cases whatsoever, either more openly or latently, the ruling principle of the sublime." And with terror usually goes some kind or degree of

147

obscurity. The Sublime, which is the true greatness of poetry, is therefore in general associated with obscurity in the idea represented : so much so that " a clear idea is another name for a little idea." It may be noted that this category of the Sublime admits ugliness as an element in poetry.

What is more important to note, however, is that this category of the Sublime is typical of Romanticism. Wherever we find Romanticism, we find the " inner " life somehow asserting its superiority over the " outer." Burke's insistence that poetry must be judged by its emotional effect is the first declaration of the rights of romantic criticism—criticism by purely subjective standards. And the romantic importance of " inner " experience over the " outer " world is further asserted by his insistence on the poetic value of obscurity in what is represented. For obscurity, like ideas of boundlessness and infinitude, sets the mind free to expand its inner powers unconditioned by the outer actuality of things. It is thus that, for romanticism, " distance lends enchantment to the view " : distance obscures, actuality becomes vague, and in its place

Fancy " glows divinely there." It is scarcely necessary to observe that the opposite of Romanticism is Realism, which puts all its emphasis on the " outer " world. But realism, in the tradition of critical method, has never been anything like so important as romanticism.

Kant, in the *Critique of Judgement*, agrees with Burke that the Sublime and the Beautiful are distinct categories in the æsthetic judgement ; but seems to think that the pleasure in the Sublime consists in the mind's recovery from the imminent overwhelming force of natural grandeur : by collecting all its strength to resist the overpowering effect of sublime landscape, the mind is invigorated by its sense of asserting its moral superiority over Nature. Kant thought much more of the æsthetic judgement in scenery than in art ; but his discussion of the Sublime in Nature combined with Burke's treatment of the Sublime in art to enlarge the range of æsthetic experience : thereby, of course, greatly enriching the tradition of criticism.

Less closely connected with romanticism, but belonging to the same line of criticism as Burke and Kant, *Lessing*, in his famous essay on the statuary group

known as *Laokoön*,[1] considers the relations
of literature with the graphic arts. Lessing easily admits, with Burke, that the
ugly may successfully be introduced into
poetry ; but this is because he limits more
narrowly even than Burke the scope and
meaning of beauty. Beauty is the ideal of
the graphic arts ; but for poetry, expressiveness is the ideal : and ugliness may be
very expressive. On the contrary beauty,
which is given by shapeliness of visible
form, may be destroyed by expressiveness.
What Virgil's poetry can artistically do in
describing Laokoön's horrible death, cannot be artistically done by the sculptor
who represents the same incident in visible
form. It is doubtful whether the facts bear
out this particular argument ; but it leads
Lessing to a very important conclusion.

The difference of effect between poetry
and graphic art is due to the difference in
the way they present their subjects, which
again is due to the difference of their
media. Owing to the medium of painting
or sculpture, graphic art is the static representation of objects in single moments of
their existence ; whereas poetry, again
owing to its medium, must be the

:Translated in Bohn's Library (Bell).

successive representation of actions in a continuous sequence of existence. Lessing refers to an old Greek saying, attributed to Simonides, that painting is dumb poetry, poetry is speaking painting. This emphasizes the resemblance between the arts ; but the difference between them is equally important. Painting must never seek to do what only literature can do, literature never what painting only can do. But perhaps Lessing did not perceive how radical was the distinction he maintained : later criticism has also sometimes failed to perceive this. When a picture is said to "tell a story," does it really compete with literature ? How can literature present its subject in actual colour and form ? So, too, description in poetry cannot really trespass on the domain of painting. But Lessing did invaluable service to criticism by emphasizing the boundaries dividing the arts. For whatever an art can do is conditioned by the medium in which it is done ; and the rules which genuinely formulate what can be done and what cannot be done in this medium or in that, are necessarily rules of an absolute validity.

The great contribution of romanticism

151

to the tradition of criticism lies in the liberty of interpretation which it claims. This liberty denies the validity of the so-called objective rules of a merely pedantic classicism, but easily accepts the genuinely objective rules which, as Lessing showed, may be founded on the nature of the artistic medium ; for these latter rules do not in the least interfere with purely subjective judgement. It was romanticism that made possible the critical individualism, the complete liberty of appreciation, in Lamb, Coleridge, and Hazlitt. The danger is, the encouragement romanticism gives to irresponsibility. But the last word in the theory of romantic criticism, the perfectly balanced summation of the claims of liberty and responsibility, is given by Manzoni's formula in his preface to his noble poem *Il Conte di Carmagnola*. Every composition contains within itself the rules by which it should be criticized, or, as Manzoni himself more carefully puts it, " offers to anyone who wishes to examine it the principles necessary to form a judgement of it." These principles may be obtained by asking three questions: What was the author's intention ? Was the intention reasonable ? Has the author

carried it out ? In other words : *Discover*
the purpose ; *judge* its worth ; *criticize* the
technique. This puts Manzoni's meaning
in the most general form possible, but
introduces a slight modification of it.
It may be said, that in this there is
nothing essentially romantic. And that is
true : Manzoni's great dictum is only
historically romantic. It was uttered as a
protest against the doctrine of universal
abstract standards in criticism, to which
false classicism and misapplied rationalism
had perverted the teaching of Aristotle,
Horace, and " Longinus." Having exploded that doctrine, Manzoni's formula
becomes not merely a statement of the
ideals of romantic criticism, but indicates
the procedure of all sane criticism whatsoever.

V: CONCLUSION

V. CONCLUSION

WITH MANZONI's wisdom, we may conclude. The pronouncement concerns criticism, not theory. Every work of art is a particular case, and must be judged as such ; and the judgement must be of its merit. But the dictum is not quite so simple as it looks. How are we to know what an author's *intentions* are ? An author seldom tells us that, and when he does, his information is seldom to be trusted. For the reason why a work of art exists at all is, that it was the only way in which its author could truly give us his intentions. What he may say of them elsewhere will surely be more or less than, or beside, the truth. But if we allow the work of art to make its effect on us as a whole, then in that final unity of its total impression we have the author's intention so far as we are able to respond to it. This is universally true of art ; and it is a truth established not by criticism, but by the theory of art. Thus Manzoni's first critical principle is quite ineffective by itself, but

157

becomes everything Manzoni intended it
to be when it is based on theoretical principles. Precisely the same is true of the
third part of his dictum. It is here that
the paraphrase given above slightly modi-
fies Manzoni's meaning. For if we know the
author's intentions, we only do so because
he has, somehow or other, carried them
out. The real question is, *How* has he
carried them out ? But criticism of technique is helpless without understanding of
the general nature and function of technique, which only the theory of art can
provide.

All this applies to the whole history of
criticism. The rules of criticism, so far as
they are valid, are nothing but modes of
using universal theory in particular cases.
They are thus objective rules ; and criticism, by virtue of them, need not wholly
depend on the personal peculiarity of the
critic. But the subjective element must
come in. For it is entirely for its own purpose that criticism uses theory, a purpose
which, strictly speaking, theory cannot
assist : namely, to judge of merit. Obviously, nothing can limit the rights of
purely subjective judgement on the question of merit. But as regards technique, if

the criticism is at all considerable, the subjective judgement will be combined with judgement as certainly objective ; for here criticism must have regard to rules— not rules laid down by mere authority, but rules derived from the very nature of art, made available by æsthetic theory. There remains the second principle in Manzoni's threefold dictum : the worth of the poet's inspiration. The judgement here can be nothing but entirely subjective, and its freedom is absolute. Nevertheless, the value of the critic's judgement in this respect does not depend on its freedom ; it depends on the worth of the critic. When he is judging of technique, the weight of his verdict will largely be given by his intellectual qualities. But when he is judging of inspiration, the value of his judgement will depend on the whole man, on his moral and temperamental character, as well as his brain.

BIBLIOGRAPHICAL NOTE

G. SAINTSBURY : *History of Criticism* ; 3 Vols. (London. 1902)

J. E. SPINGARN : *History of Literary Criticism in the Renaissance* (New York and Oxford. 1912)

H. B. CHARLTON : *Castlevetro's Theory of Poetry* (Manchester. 1913)

B. A. GREENING LAMBORN : *Rudiments of Criticism* (Oxford. 1916)

G. GREGORY SMITH : *Elizabethan Critical Essays* (Oxford. 1904)

R. A. SCOTT-JAMES : *The Making of Literature* (London. 1930)

J. E. SPINGARN : *Seventeenth Century Critical Essays* (Oxford. 1908)
Creative Criticism (New York. 1917 ; Oxford. 1926)

J. SHAWCROSS : *Coleridge's Biographia Literaria* ; 2 Vols. (Oxford. 1907)

A. C. BRADLEY : *Oxford Lectures on Poetry* (London. 1909)

J. MIDDLETON MURRY : *The Problem of Style* (Oxford. 1922)

JOHN LIVINGSTONE LOWES : *Convention and Revolt in Poetry* (New York. 1919 ; Oxford. 1930)

GEORGE EDWARD WOODBERRY : *Inspiration of Poetry* (New York. 1910)

WALTER PATER : *Appreciations* (" Style ") (London. 1889)

MATTHEW ARNOLD : *Essays in Criticism* ; 1st Series : (" Function of Criticism ") (London. 1865)